Words Aptly Spoken®
AMERICAN LITERATURE
a companion guide to classic literature

SECOND EDITION

compiled and edited by Jen Greenholt

MULTIMEDIA

Jen Greenholt, *Words Aptly Spoken*® Series
A Companion Guide to Classic Literature, American Literature
First edition printed 2007. Second edition printed 2011.

Published by Classical Conversations, Inc.
P.O. Box 909
West End, NC 27376
www.ClassicalConversations.com | www.ClassicalConversationsBooks.com

Cover design by Classical Conversations. Cover image courtesy of Library of Congress, *"Mark Twain," America's best humorist*, LC-USZC4-4294.

Printed in the United States of America.

ISBN: 978-0-9829845-0-5

Acknowledgments

Many thanks to Pam Greenholt for her input and suggestions on the writing practice sections; to the editors at Classical Conversations for making this book the best it can be; and to Classical Conversations for giving me the opportunity to spend so many hours with these classic American authors.

Foreword

This collection introduces you to twenty-nine works of American literature from early Christian sermons to twentieth-century plays. As a bonus, the book includes the text of three sermons by Christian ministers from early America, two stories by the great storyteller O. Henry, and two poems by the classic American poet Henry Wadsworth Longfellow.

While reading these classic works, take time to engage with the author. What hard questions does the book ask you to consider? Remember, you don't have to agree with the author in order to benefit from a book. Sometimes you learn just as much by disagreeing, because the experience forces you a) to think through the reasons you disagree, and b) to strengthen your own beliefs in the process.

As with the other collections in the *Words Aptly Spoken* series, *American Literature* contains a series of questions about each work. Review Questions ensure that you understand the basic plot, characters, setting, and message of the book. Thought Questions take the themes and ideas raised by each author and help you apply them to other, more familiar situations.

In the field of literature, reading and writing are closely tied. *American Literature* helps you make this connection by walking you step-by-step through the process of writing an essay about literature. Each work you will study is accompanied by a writing practice section that targets the important skills you need to have in order to write a good essay about literature.

As you read and write your way through these classics of American literature, make it your goal to be critical in the best sense of the word. Remember, every author in this collection was a person who was flawed, biased, and opinionated.

By reading and writing about these individuals and remaining, as you do so, aware that they were human, you should not lose appreciation for what they accomplished. Instead, you should recognize that their imperfect contributions have helped to shape American thought in the past just as your contributions can help shape future thought.

Best wishes, and happy reading!

Table of Contents

A Note For Parents: Tools for the Journey

If you have ever heard Shakespeare performed before a live audience and marveled at the ease with which the words flowed from the actors' lips; if you have ever envied people who can call on Milton, Dickens, Joyce, and Lewis to lend eloquence to their argument; if you have skimmed a list of the hundred greatest novels of all time and winced as you remembered struggling to finish *The Grapes of Wrath* in high school—you may think that the great conversations of literature are forever closed to you.

The good news is, they're not! Whether you are a student, an adult, a parent, a child, or all of the above, you have the capability to train yourself not only to read great literature, but also to share its beauty, truth, and joy with others.

Although most people learn to read as children, the art of deliberately engaging with the content and ideas of a novel or short story requires ongoing practice.

The *Words Aptly Spoken* series is based on the classical model of education,[1] which breaks learning into three natural stages: grammar, dialectic, and rhetoric. In the grammar stage, you learn the vocabulary of a subject. In the dialectic stage, you learn to develop logical arguments and analyze others' ideas. In the rhetoric stage, you explore the consequences of ideas as you form and express your own. This guide will help you as you begin to apply the classical model to the study of literature.

Why American Literature?

American literature is a varied and exciting field. Every century, America has undergone many social, cultural, economic, and political changes. These changes have had a significant influence on the way authors have written and what they have written about. In addition, these changes have made American literature an excellent source for competing ideas.

As you become more comfortable with the grammar of reading—plot, characters, setting, conflict, etc.—you should begin to read for ideas, so you can engage with those ideas and wrestle through their implications. In many ways, reading is an exchange of ideas between the author and the reader, like two friends sitting down in front of a fire to discuss the secrets of life.

After the fire has died, it is up to you to decide what happens next. Do you put aside the questions and the new thoughts? Or do you daily go back to those lessons and apply them to your life? The decision is yours. Learning to write about these books and the ideas they contain (**rhetoric**) is the next step toward sharing your ideas and conclusions with the people around you.

How to Use This Book

Despite popular belief, reading is not wholly instinctive. Because comprehension, analysis, and critical thinking require practice, each work of literature you will study is broken down by chapter into a series of questions designed to give structure and guidance to your reading.

---

[1] See Dorothy Sayers' essay, "The Lost Tools of Learning."

Although the questions are arranged chapter-by-chapter, most readers will not pause to answer questions after finishing a chapter. If the book has captured your imagination the way classic literature ought to, you won't want to stop reading! For this reason, treat these questions as tools not only for reading, but also for writing, leading discussion, and sharing your ideas with others.

Review Questions pull out the **grammar** for each chapter: Who is the book about? (Characters) What happens? (Plot) Where does it take place? (Setting) What is the message? (Theme) What is the scope or time frame? (Focus) For readers of all ages, repeatedly asking these questions will generate good reading habits; eventually, as you read, your brain will automatically take note of this information and store it for future use.

Thought Questions are an exercise in **dialectic**, taking the basic elements from the Review Questions and encouraging you to analyze that information in light of other knowledge. As you become more familiar with the building blocks of a story, you should begin to ask questions of your own. What does this mean for me? How should I respond to this argument? You can use the Thought Questions to jump-start your own thinking process, as training tools for leading discussion, or as topics for essays.

If you cannot answer some of the questions by the time you have finished the book, consider going back and re-reading sections you may only have skimmed the first time. A word of caution: don't merely "look up" the answers to the questions and skim the rest of the book. Once established, this habit will make it harder for you to read and understand more difficult books. After all, self-respecting Olympic runners know that they would be at a severe disadvantage in the actual games if they secretly completed only half of their daily training regimen. In the same way, the results you achieve as a reader will reflect the quality and consistency of your training.

Because measuring progress is a part of learning, each section in this book begins or ends with suggested reading or writing exercises that allow you to gauge how well you have mastered the skills you've been practicing. Although a particular exercise for writing is suggested with each book studied, you can rearrange and revise to suit your needs.

It is best if you have your own copy of each book so you can highlight or make notes in the margins. If, however, you need to use a copy belonging to the library or to a friend, consider reading with a small notebook or a pad of sticky notes nearby so you can jot down ideas and connections while they are fresh in your head.

The Journey in Perspective

One of the most important things to remember as you start—or resume—this journey is that it doesn't happen overnight. The art of leading and sharing in conversations about classical literature takes a lifetime to refine. You must begin with the fundamentals: learning to read closely, taking notes, and developing the vocabulary to structure your ideas and explain them to others (**grammar**). You must practice: adding new techniques, revising old ones, and comparing the results (**dialectic**). And then you will be ready to start all over again as you share the joy of the journey with others around you (**rhetoric**). Let's get started!

Reading Skills

Being a good reader takes practice, and it is vital to a range of other skills. If you miss the big ideas when you read, you cannot analyze or critique those ideas, identify the underlying messages, or respond to them thoughtfully in writing or conversation. These tips will help you read more effectively.

Vocabulary

If you see an unfamiliar word, take a minute to look up the definition and write it down. Not only will this improve your vocabulary, but it will help you avoid missing important details. Pay particular attention to words that have a different connotation now than they had when the book was written.

Characters

Keep a list of the main characters. Write down their names, a few defining characteristics, and their relationships with other characters. If you find a section that shows their character traits especially well, write down the page number.

Plot

Write down a skeletal outline of the book's plot. What happened, to whom, when, where, and how? Focus on turning points and revelations that were important to the plot's development.

Timeline

Keep a timeline of the major events in the book. This is especially useful if multiple subplots take place at the same time. You can also use a timeline to keep track of flashbacks or dream sequences.

Themes

Do you see a pattern in the problems that plague the characters? Is there some flaw that all the main characters share? Write it down. Also, if something in the book reminds you of another book or story you have read, jot down the page number(s) and the element(s) that seem similar.

Quotes

Does a character say something memorable? Underline or highlight it, or write down the page number and a few key words. When you write about or discuss the book, you will need evidence, and it is much easier to mark quotes as you go than to relocate specific passages when you need them.

Don't forget to read with a notebook or pad of sticky notes handy. If you own the book, margins are a great place to write, but make sure you use a bookmark so you can find your notes. Keep practicing these reading skills, and you will find your jobs as thinker, critic, and writer much easier as a result.

About the Essay

Reading and writing go hand in hand. A good book is meant to be shared, and essays are one way of sharing your thoughts about a book with others. Essays come in many different forms and have many different purposes. As you study the books in this guide, try your hand at the essay styles listed below. Being able to write more than one kind of essay will improve your writing technique, keep you interested and engaged, and help you look at literature with new perspective.

Book report

The first type of essay many students encounter is the book report. Although the implied reader of a book report is someone who wants to find out more about the book, the main purpose of writing a book report is to demonstrate that the writer has read the book, understands the basic elements of the story, and has formed an opinion about the book's merits.

Book reports are all about learning and repeating the **grammar** of literature. Writing a book report is a little bit like writing a newspaper article. A book report should answer the journalistic questions who – what – why – when – where – how. Your focus is on facts and important characters and plot points, not on details or in-depth analysis.

The first paragraph should introduce the author and the book, including the main characters and the setting. The next few paragraphs should lay out the plot, focusing on the big events and how they are related. The final paragraph should briefly analyze and judge the merits of the book. Each section of the essay should include support in the form of quotations from the book.

Think about this type of writing as the foundation for more complex essays. As with reading, when you practice summarizing the plot, characters, conflict, and resolution of a book, your brain is developing the habit of identifying these core elements. Later, you will be able to write with ease about not just the names of the characters but also their relationship to each other as they develop and change.

Character sketch

Character sketches are a good example of the next stage in your development as a writer. A character sketch asks you to pick out the important information relating to a particular character. In this way, like book reports, character sketches are more about description than argument. Unlike book reports, however, character sketches require you to draw on your own interpretations of the character's actions in order to write the essay. You will need to analyze the grammar of the book and begin to draw logical conclusions about it (**dialectic**).

In a character sketch, you will introduce your reader to one of the book's characters by presenting details from the book that support your overall impression of the character. You can use the character's words, interactions with other characters, actions, and thoughts (if available) to help you "sketch" your character. When you write a character sketch, remember to *show* rather than *tell*. For example, instead of telling your reader that "Jane Doe was an insecure person," you could describe a scene in which Jane was given a compliment but was convinced that it was spoken sarcastically.

The first paragraph should introduce the character and his/her relationship to the plot. The next few paragraphs should use examples and quotes to highlight a particular aspect of the character's personality. In other words, you should begin to show your reader who this person is and how you have come to that conclusion. The final paragraph should either point back to the character's impact on the plot or remind readers how the character changes or grows over the course of the book.

Book critique

Another type of essay that builds your dialectic skills is the book critique. A book critique is similar to a book report in that it briefly describes the book. A critique, however, goes one step further to analyze how well the grammar of the book works together to produce a cohesive whole.

A critique is not an unsupported statement of your opinion about the book. Some book reports, albeit not especially good ones, tend to gush, "This was a great book; I loved reading it, and I will recommend it to all my friends." That type of writing may be appropriate to a book report, but a critique asks you to explain the reasons behind your opinion.

In a book critique, you should analyze the effectiveness of the book as a piece of writing. Were the characters believable? Why or why not? Did the plot conclude logically or did it ask readers to disregard logic? Was the dialogue slow? Were there too many descriptions? For this task, the grammar of reading is extremely important because you have to be able to identify the author's techniques for developing characters and structuring the plot in order to critique why they did not work as intended.

The first paragraph of a book critique should introduce the book and its author and briefly summarize the plot. The next few paragraphs should identify the book's strengths and weaknesses, using examples and quotes to support your claims. The final paragraph should pass judgment on the book as a whole. This is your chance to explain what the author could have done better.

The most difficult part about writing a book critique is to keep your tone professional even as you point out examples of poor writing, jumbled plot, and one-dimensional characters. If you were presenting your essay to the author of the book, you would not want to tell him/her that the book "had no plot whatsoever." You might, however, be able to tactfully mention that, "the book's focus on character rather than plot made the transition to a battle scene in chapter four seem abrupt." Your writing should reflect similar preciseness and avoid *ad hominem*[2] attacks on the author.

Critical essay

Critical essays are by far the most common type of academic writing in upper-level literature classes. In addition, because this type of essay asks you to consider the book in greater depth as you develop an argument about the ideas it contains, critical essays are an important step from the dialectic stage, in which you analyze others' writing and arguments,

---

[2]Latin for "to the man", an *ad hominem* attack is a logical fallacy committed when someone attacks the character of the person making an argument rather than responding to the argument itself.

toward the **rhetoric** stage, in which you will develop and present your own ideas. For these reasons, the writing practice sections in this book will focus mainly on planning and writing critical essays.

Before you can plunge into the writing process, however, you must go back to the grammar in order to avoid a common misperception about the nature of a critical essay. The word "critical" may be misleading. Although "critical" and "critique" are similar words, they are used in two different ways in this context. A critique, as mentioned earlier, is intended to find fault with a book. Its purpose is to pick out weaknesses in the author's writing style or development of plot and character.

A critical essay, by contrast, focuses on the reader's insight into the book. Think of "critical" as it is used in the phrase "critical thinking." To think about something critically is to question it rather than to absorb it without considering the implications. A critical essay should look below the surface of the book. Your essay could highlight a connection between several books, find and analyze a significant moment in a character's development, or trace a repeated theme of the book and discuss the consequences of that idea.

No matter which approach you choose, you will build critical essays on an argument or claim you make about the book. That claim is called a **thesis**. The next section will focus on how to select a thesis and write a critical essay. For now, just remember that a critical essay is first and foremost about *your* thoughts. It is impossible to write a critical essay without a) reading the book, and b) engaging your mind on the level of ideas as you do so. Before you think about writing the essay, you must always begin by thinking about the book.

Brain Work
PLANNING THE ESSAY

Before you even begin to write, it is important to think about what you want to say. Planning helps you organize and makes the job easier when you actually begin to write. The planning phase can be broken down into five or six steps: asking a question, developing a thesis, building an argument, preparing an outline, sometimes conducting research, and thinking about form and style. Of course, all of these steps are possible only after you have read the book at least once.

Asking a question

The first few steps of pre-writing involve narrowing down your interests from the broad scope, to a general topic, to a specific question. Start by asking a few basic questions about your interests.

- Do you want to talk about the story within the book, or do you want to relate the book to outside information?

- If you chose to stay within the text, are you interested in the plot and characters, or do you want to look at the author's themes or the characters' philosophies?

- If you chose to look outside the text, do you want to talk about historical events, cultural attitudes, or events in the author's life as they relate to the book?[3]

Now that you've narrowed down the scope of your paper, look back at your notes. What topics interested you while you were reading? Did a particular character fascinate you? Did you see a lot of comparisons between the author's and the protagonist's lives? Decide on a general topic based on this information.

A strong argument about literature responds to a problem, puzzle, or question raised by the book. Once you have a topic, choose a question you would like to answer. For example, if you were writing an essay about *The Secret Garden*, you might be interested in the themes of the book, particularly the theme of love. Within that topic, you might be curious about the characters' understanding of what love means. You might ask the following question: What is Archibald Craven's concept of love, and how does it change by the end of the book?

Developing a thesis

A thesis is your answer to the question you have asked. It is the claim you will make about the book. Developing a thesis is one of the most important parts of writing a critical essay, so at this point, you may want to go back and re-read sections of the book that deal with your

---

[3]Use caution with this last option: remember that what an author writes is separate from—though influenced by—who he or she is. It's risky to assume that everything in an author's books lines up with an experience in his or her life.

topic. You should build your claim from the book rather than trying to manipulate the book to fit your claim.

Your goal should be to make an argument that is somewhere between the obvious and the unsupportable. On one hand, it is very difficult to argue something that is self-evident. You wouldn't have a very good argument if you walked up to someone and said, "I think there are twelve months in a year, and I'm going to prove it." The other person would be likely to walk away. However, if you said, "I think I can prove there should be only ten months in a year," you could have a very interesting conversation. For this reason, steering clear of claims that are too obvious is one objective.

On the other hand, you will need to have reasonable support for your thesis. Your argument should interpret and tie together the quotes and actions of characters in the book. You should be able to logically argue in favor of your thesis using quotations from the book. It's worth repeating that your thesis should come out of the book; the book shouldn't be forced into it.

In the example from *Secret Garden*, you might develop the following thesis: Archibald Craven initially thinks love and material gifts are the same thing, but by the end of the book he realizes that love is different and more important.

Building an argument

Once you have a thesis, the next step is to lay out your argument. What steps are necessary to convince your reader to accept your thesis? In order to visualize those steps, it is helpful to lay out your argument point-by-point. As an illustration, consider this word game:

To play, take one word, and then, by changing one letter at a time, turn it into another word with the same number of letters. For example: FISH ⇨HOOK. Here is one possible solution:

> FISH ⇨ FIST ⇨ FAST ⇨ CAST ⇨ COST ⇨ COLT ⇨ BOLT ⇨ BOOT ⇨ HOOT ⇨ HOOK

If you merely skipped from FISH to HOOK, you would have proven nothing. In order for the game to work, each link must lead logically from the last, but there may be multiple ways to reach the same conclusion. The same "rules" apply to your essay. At each step, your reader should be able to follow your line of reasoning without having to make leaps in logic.

For the sample thesis from *The Secret Garden*, you would need to prove that Archibald Craven originally thought love and material comforts were the same thing, and that he later realized love was different. To do that, you would need to provide examples in which Mr. Craven tries to show love by buying gifts for his son, Colin, or his niece, Mary. Next, you would need to show a cause for his change of thinking: for example, a conversation with another character. Finally, you would need to give examples from the end of the book, in which he tries to show a different kind of love that is separate from gift giving.

Preparing an outline

Building an argument leads naturally into preparing an outline. Once you have the step-by-step process for proving your thesis, you can turn that mental path into an outline. Your outline can be as broad or as detailed as you want; however, a more detailed outline will make your job easier when you start writing. This is a good time to start thinking about the scenes or events in the book that you will use to back up your argument.

Here is one possible outline for the sample topic:

I.   Introduction

II. Mr. Craven's initial relationships (emphasizing the connection between love and gifts)
     A. With Mary
        1. Love
        2. Gifts
     B. With Colin
        1. Love
        2. Gifts

III. Mr. Craven's change of mind
     A. Conversations with Mary
     B. Conversation with Mrs. Sowerby

IV. Mr. Craven's new relationships (emphasizing that the two types of affection are separate)
     A. With Mary
        1. Love
        2. Gifts
     B. With Colin
        1. Love
        2. Gifts

V.   Conclusion

Conducting research

If you take a logic or debate class, you will learn that the difference between a shouting match and a logical argument can be as simple as the use of evidence. Any argument will be stronger if you can back it up with proof. In literary studies, support comes in two forms. First, you can use **primary support**, which comes from the book you are writing about. If you are writing an essay about *The Secret Garden*, your primary support will be quotes from *The Secret Garden*. Most of your primary research will take place as you read and think about your argument, before you even begin to write.

At this point in your writing, you will probably rely mostly on primary support, using quotes from the book to back up your opinions. In some cases, however, you may begin to write about a topic and discover after you create your outline that you will need **secondary support**.

Secondary support comes from books or journal articles that other scholars have written about your book or topic. If you are writing about historical events or social conditions at the time a book was written, you may need to consult an outside source to find information about, for example, nineteenth-century slavery laws or the principles of the transcendental movement in philosophy.

If you are asked to find research to support your ideas, it is important to know where to look. Through the Internet, an abundance of information is available. Be cautious, however. Writing a good essay is not possible unless you use credible information. The Internet contains a lot of good information, but it also contains a lot of information that is biased or just plain untrue. Always check the credentials of your sources, especially online sources. Books or articles written by professors or researchers are much more credible than blogs or websites that can be edited by anyone.

If you are in doubt, remember that the library is always a good place to search. Published books and journal articles (with some exceptions) go through a rigorous editing process by experts in the field, which means they are less likely to contain errors or unsupported claims. In addition, your librarian may be able to give you advice about finding credible information.

Thinking about form and style

Although an essay is largely about your thoughts and interpretation, it should still be professionally written. That means writing in third person when possible (not using I, me, you, or we) and using formal language and style (no contractions, slang terms, or colloquialisms).

In a critical essay, it may be difficult to avoid inserting judgments about the characters and plot of the book. It is acceptable to use firm words and make decisive statements about a book. In fact, an essay that is too hesitant and qualifies every statement with "maybe" or "one might think" is as bad as an essay that is too forceful. Just remember to back up your claims with examples and evidence from the book.

When you first sit down to write, it is not important to get everything just right. You will make mistakes and need to make changes—that's why you revise your paper after you finish—but if you keep these principles in mind as you write and practice them consistently, the professional voice you develop will become more natural and personal.

Hand Work
WRITING THE ESSAY

After you have put in all the hard work of pre-writing, actually beginning to write may come as something of a relief. Rather than writing a sentence, stopping, and trying to figure out where to go next, you already have a plan to which you can refer if you get stuck. Now all you have to do is to transfer the ideas in your head onto the page.

Writing a rough draft

When you begin to write, focus on getting your ideas down on paper. There will be plenty of time later to go back and proofread. Keep your outline and notes beside you as you write. Depending on the length of the paper, you should aim to write one or more paragraphs for each section of your outline. Because you're making a claim about a book, each section of your paper should include at least one supporting quote or reference from that book.

Some people prefer to write sections as the inspiration comes to them, and then they organize the paper after they finish. Others start at the beginning and write straight through to the end. Either method is okay, but each one has a few pitfalls to avoid.

The risk of writing section-by-section is that your paper will lack continuity because it has been written out of order and stitched together. If you write this way, when you finish, go back and read the transitions between sections. Do they flow without a noticeable break? Your goal is for someone who has never seen your outline to be able to follow your logic.

The danger of writing straight through is that you will lose sight of your thesis as you follow your train of thought. If you write this way, when you finish, read your introduction and conclusion back-to-back. Do they "match up"? Readers should not expect that you will talk about one thing based on your introduction only to find that you've actually led them to another, unrelated conclusion.

Regardless of which method you choose, always pay special attention to your introduction and conclusion. These are some of the most important sections of your paper, and sometimes it is easier to write—or at least revise—them after you finish the body of the paper.

Refining the introduction

From the very beginning, the introduction should catch your reader's attention and give him or her a reason to keep reading. In your first sentence, you might use a provocative question, a poignant quote, or a strong statement—all examples of a good "hook"—to do so. Next, your introduction should present the general topic of the paper. Finally, it should contain two important pieces: your thesis and a brief "road map." (See "Brain Work" for a discussion of the thesis.)

Your road map should be 1-2 sentences long. Think of a road map as a miniature outline that gives your reader a sense of direction and leads up to your thesis. For example, "This paper examines Mr. Craven's relationships with Mary and Colin early in the book and contrasts them with his interactions at the end of the book. In each situation, the essay compares Mr. Craven's demonstrations of love to his gift giving." Then, when you transition into the body of your paper, your readers will know what the major steps in your argument will be.

Revising the conclusion

If the introduction of the paper presents a miniature version of your argument and prepares the reader for the rest of the paper, the conclusion presents a recap of your argument and then offers the reader a chance to respond.

The first goal of your conclusion is to review the major points you have made and remind the reader how you have proven your thesis. Try not to repeat yourself; instead, pull out the most important details and show your reader how your thesis makes sense of them. Then, your conclusion should end with a memorable thought or quotation that goes one step further to suggest what the broader implications of your argument might be.

Perhaps your claim has consequences for the way people read this particular book or categorize this author. Maybe your argument will affect the way readers interpret a character or scene. Or perhaps, thinking critically about a book's theme could influence the way people relate to others around them. This is your chance to practice **rhetoric**, to persuade your readers that ideas have consequences.

Choosing a title

The title of your essay is the first thing readers will see. As such, it should tell the reader what your essay is about, but it should do so in a memorable way. A title like *"The Secret Garden*: An Essay" will not make your potential readers excited about what you have to say. On the other hand, "Growing Love in *The Secret Garden*" might encourage someone to read further.

A title can be uninformative because it is too vague, but a title that is flashy with no substance is equally unhelpful. Your title needs to give the reader a sense of what the essay is about. As with your writing style, it should be professional in tone. Remember, you should draw the reader in with your ideas, not just your ability to create puns or play with words.

Proofreading

Once the initial writing is complete, it is time to edit your essay. It is easiest to start with the biggest changes and move to the smaller ones. If you proofread for grammar, then decide you need to rewrite the entire middle section, you will have to check for grammar errors again when you are finished.

The first thing to evaluate is content. Does your paper fulfill your assignment? If not, you may have to rewrite or at least alter your essay so it fits the assigned task. Does the body of your paper prove your thesis? If not, go back and make those important links, showing the reader exactly why your thesis is correct. Does the paper use the book for support? If not, go back and cut out generalizations, replacing them with evidence.

Moving from the paper as a whole to the level of paragraphs, the next thing you should look for is organization. Your paper should make sense and smoothly develop your argument. One way to check organization is to create an outline **from** your paper. Write down the main point of each paragraph in one sentence or less. Look at these topic sentences in the order that they appear in your paper. Do they make sense? Do they follow a logical order? If not, rearrange the sentences, then rearrange the corresponding paragraphs in your paper.

Now you need to make sure you have smooth transitions between your paragraphs. You want to make it easy for your reader to follow your train of thought. If you have just finished talking about one character's development, you should not jump straight into a paragraph about the turning point in the plot. Instead, you should use a transition sentence to link these two ideas. For example, "[Character's] changes start a chain of events that alters the entire plot of the book."

The next two steps, which move to the sentence level, may overlap to some extent. First, check for clarity. The most efficient way to find out if your paper is clear is to have someone else read it aloud. If you cannot find someone, read the paper aloud to yourself. Are your sentences smooth or choppy? Are your quotes smoothly integrated? Most importantly, this is the time to make sure your paper says what you want it to say.

When you are satisfied that the paper is clear, look for grammatical errors and errors in spelling or word choice. Try to avoid contractions (isn't, don't, can't) and first-person (I, me, we) or second-person pronouns (you). Go back and review information about punctuation and capitalization. Check for run-on sentences and fragments. Make sure your subjects and verbs and your nouns and pronouns agree in number. Check for consistency in your verb tenses. Watch for commonly-confused words (their, there, and they're; its and it's).

Finally, double-check your citations and use of research, making sure you have given proper credit and formatted your citations according to MLA or other guidelines. This last step may involve familiarizing yourself with some new **grammar** specific to academic writing.

Formatting citations

Writers and researchers put a lot of time into their work, and they deserve recognition for that effort. When you use someone else's ideas or information, failure to give proper credit is called plagiarism.[4] Plagiarism includes copying and pasting information from the Internet, paraphrasing or directly quoting someone else's words without giving them credit, and claiming someone else's ideas as your own. Plagiarism is a serious academic offense and may result in failure of an assignment or a class. Even more importantly, plagiarism is unethical. It means that instead of doing your own work, you took someone else's and pretended it was yours.

There are several ways to use research correctly. You can use an author's words exactly, but you must use quotation marks. You can also paraphrase the author's words. Paraphrasing does not mean simply changing a word or two; it means completely rewriting the information in your own words and sentence structure. Whether you paraphrase or quote, you must include citations. Since this book is about literary writing, you should use the format of the

---

[4]The word "plagiarism" comes from the Latin verb *plagiare*, to kidnap.

Modern Language Association (MLA). MLA style has two parts: in-text (parenthetical) citations and a bibliography.

In-text citations appear in the body of the paper. After using information or a direct quotation, put the author's last name and the page number in parentheses, with no punctuation in between. For example, "This book is a classic" (Smith 101). Notice that the final quotation mark comes **before** the in-text citation and the punctuation mark comes **after** the citation. One exception is if the punctuation affects the mood of the quote. The most common examples are an exclamation point or a question mark. For example, Jane Doe exclaims, "Are we lost?" (Author 92).

The in-text citation points your reader to the bibliography, where complete information is given for each author referenced. The bibliography in MLA is called a "Works Cited" page. Entries are alphabetized by the author's last name (to match the in-text citation). See Figure 1 below for examples of different types of sources in MLA format. The basic format for a works cited entry is:

Book
Author's last name, first name. *Title*.[5] Publisher's location: Publisher's name, Year published.

Journal Article
Author's last name, first name. "Title." *Journal Title*. Volume.Issue (Date): Page range.

Website
Author's last name, first name. "Title of page." Sponsor (Date written). Accessed (Date) from [URL].

Figure 1

	Works Cited page	**In Text**
Book	Mills, John. *My Book*. New York: Random House, 1992.	(Mills 28)
Book, 2+ authors	Jeffers, Anne and David Miller. *Their Book*. London: Pearson, 2001.	(Jeffers and Miller 3)
Work in an anthology	Green, Terry. "His Article." *Collected Book*. Ed.[6] Tim Roe. New York: Scribes, 2005. 54-61.	(Green 58)
Newspaper	Harris, Tom. "Big News." *The Washington Post* 14 May 2004, A2.	(Harris A2)
Journal	Brown, Alice. "Her Article." *Literary Journal*. 35.4 (1998): 13-21.	(Brown 14)
Website	Dennis, George. "His Web Text." Research Foundation (2005). Accessed 4/14/2007 from [http://www.research.org/webtext].	(Dennis)

---

[5]If you are citing from a stand-alone work (a book or play), use italics for the title. If it is not published separately (a poem or short story), use quotation marks around the title.

[6]In an anthology, the abbreviation "Ed." is short for "editor," the person who compiled the anthology.

Work with no author	"About Literature." Literature Forum Online (2003). Accessed 5/29/2007 from [http://www.lfo.org/about].	("About")

For more detailed information about citation formats, look at the MLA Handbook, which is available at your local library or bookstore. You can also search online for MLA format.

"The Gift of the Magi"
O. Henry

William Sydney Porter (1862-1910) was in his mid-twenties, working in a bank in Texas, when he began to write satire for local newspapers. Soon after that, he was charged with embezzlement and fled to Honduras. When he returned, he spent three years in prison, during which he continued to write and publish short stories under various pen names. He became best known by the name O. Henry. After his release, he continued to write until his death. His short stories reflect his diverse experiences and are recognizable for their unusual twists and surprising endings. "The Gift of the Magi" was first published in 1906, and was later included in a collection called *The Four Million*.

One dollar and eighty-seven cents. That was all. And sixty cents of it was in pennies. Pennies saved one and two at a time by bulldozing the grocer and the vegetable man and the butcher until one's cheeks burned with the silent imputation of parsimony that such close dealing implied. Three times Della counted it. One dollar and eighty-seven cents. And the next day would be Christmas.

There was clearly nothing to do but flop down on the shabby little couch and howl. So Della did it. Which instigates the moral reflection that life is made up of sobs, sniffles, and smiles, with sniffles predominating.

While the mistress of the home is gradually subsiding from the first stage to the second, take a look at the home. A furnished flat at $8 per week. It did not exactly beggar description, but it certainly had that word on the lookout for the mendicancy squad.

In the vestibule below was a letter-box into which no letter would go, and an electric button from which no mortal finger could coax a ring. Also appertaining thereunto was a card bearing the name "Mr. James Dillingham Young."

The "Dillingham" had been flung to the breeze during a former period of prosperity when its possessor was being paid $30 a week. Now, when the income was shrunk to $20, though, they were thinking seriously of contracting to a modest and unassuming D. But whenever

Mr. James Dillingham Young came home and reached his flat above he was called "Jim" and greatly hugged by Mrs. James Dillingham Young, already introduced to you as Della. Which is all very good.

Della finished her cry and attended to her cheeks with the powder rag. She stood by the window and looked out dully at a gray cat walking a gray fence in a gray backyard. Tomorrow would be Christmas Day, and she had only $1.87 with which to buy Jim a present. She had been saving every penny she could for months, with this result. Twenty dollars a week doesn't go far. Expenses had been greater than she had calculated. They always are. Only $1.87 to buy a present for Jim. Her Jim. Many a happy hour she had spent planning for something nice for him. Something fine and rare and sterling—something just a little bit near to being worthy of the honor of being owned by Jim.

There was a pier-glass between the windows of the room. Perhaps you have seen a pier-glass in an $8 flat. A very thin and very agile person may, by observing his reflection in a rapid sequence of longitudinal strips, obtain a fairly accurate conception of his looks. Della, being slender, had mastered the art.

Suddenly she whirled from the window and stood before the glass. Her eyes were shining brilliantly, but her face had lost its color within twenty seconds. Rapidly she pulled down her hair and let it fall to its full length.

Now, there were two possessions of the James Dillingham Youngs in which they both took a mighty pride. One was Jim's gold watch that had been his father's and his grandfather's. The other was Della's hair. Had the queen of Sheba lived in a flat across the airshaft, Della would have let her hair hang out the window some day to dry just to depreciate Her Majesty's jewels and gifts. Had King Solomon been the janitor with all his treasures piled up in the basement, Jim would have pulled out his watch every time he passed, just to see him pluck at his beard from envy.

So now Della's beautiful hair fell about her rippling and shining like a cascade of brown waters. It reached below her knee and made itself almost a garment for her. And then she did it up again nervously and quickly. Once she faltered for a minute and stood still while a tear or two splashed on the worn red carpet.

On went her old brown jacket; on went her old brown hat. With a whirl of skirts and with the brilliant sparkle still in her eyes, she fluttered out the door and down the stairs to the street. Where she stopped the sign read: "Mme. Sofronie. Hair Goods of All Kinds." One flight up Della ran, and collected herself, panting. Madame, large, too white, chilly, hardly looked the "Sofronie."

"Will you buy my hair?" asked Della.

"I buy hair," said Madame. "Take yer hat off and let's have a sight at the looks of it."

Down rippled the brown cascade.

"Twenty dollars," said Madame, lifting the mass with a practised hand.

"Give it to me quick," said Della.

Oh, and the next two hours tripped by on rosy wings. Forget the hashed metaphor. She was ransacking the stores for Jim's present.

She found it at last. It surely had been made for Jim and no one else. There was no other like it in any of the stores, and she had turned all of them inside out. It was a platinum fob chain simple and chaste in design, properly proclaiming its value by substance alone and not by meretricious ornamentation—as all good things should do. It was even worthy of The Watch. As soon as she saw it she knew that it must be Jim's. It was like him. Quietness and value—the description applied to both. Twenty-one dollars they took from her for it, and she hurried home with the 87 cents. With that chain on his watch Jim might be properly anxious about the time in any company. Grand as the watch was, he sometimes looked at it on the sly on account of the old leather strap that he used in place of a chain.

When Della reached home her intoxication gave way a little to prudence and reason. She got out her curling iron and lighted the gas and went to work repairing the ravages made by generosity added to love. Which is always a tremendous task, dear friends—a mammoth task. Within forty minutes her head was covered with tiny, close-lying curls that made her look wonderfully like a truant schoolboy. She looked at her reflection in the mirror long, carefully, and critically.

"If Jim doesn't kill me," she said to herself, "before he takes a second look at me, he'll say I look like a Coney Island chorus girl. But what could I do—oh! what could I do with a dollar and eighty-seven cents?"

At 7 o'clock the coffee was made and the frying-pan was on the back of the stove hot and ready to cook the chops.

Jim was never late. Della doubled the fob chain in her hand and sat on the corner of the table near the door that he always entered. Then she heard his step on the stair away down on the first flight, and she turned white for just a moment. She had a habit for saying little silent prayers about the simplest everyday things, and now she whispered: "Please God, make him think I am still pretty."

The door opened and Jim stepped in and closed it. He looked thin and very serious. Poor fellow, he was only twenty-two—and to be burdened with a family! He needed a new overcoat and he was without gloves.

Jim stopped inside the door, as immovable as a setter at the scent of quail. His eyes were fixed upon Della, and there was an expression in them that she could not read, and it terrified her. It was not anger, nor surprise, nor disapproval, nor horror, nor any of the sentiments that she had been prepared for. He simply stared at her fixedly with that peculiar expression on his face.

Della wriggled off the table and went for him.

"Jim, darling," she cried, "don't look at me that way. I had my hair cut off and sold because I couldn't have lived through Christmas without giving you a present. It'll grow out again—you won't mind, will you? I just had to do it. My hair grows awfully fast. Say 'Merry

Christmas!' Jim, and let's be happy. You don't know what a nice—what a beautiful, nice gift I've got for you."

"You've cut off your hair?" asked Jim, laboriously, as if he had not arrived at that patent fact yet even after the hardest mental labor.

"Cut it off and sold it," said Della. "Don't you like me just as well, anyhow? I'm me without my hair, ain't I?"

Jim looked about the room curiously.

"You say your hair is gone?" he said, with an air almost of idiocy.

"You needn't look for it," said Della. "It's sold, I tell you—sold and gone, too. It's Christmas Eve, boy. Be good to me, for it went for you. Maybe the hairs of my head were numbered," she went on with sudden serious sweetness, "but nobody could ever count my love for you. Shall I put the chops on, Jim?"

Out of his trance Jim seemed quickly to wake. He enfolded his Della. For ten seconds let us regard with discreet scrutiny some inconsequential object in the other direction. Eight dollars a week or a million a year—what is the difference? A mathematician or a wit would give you the wrong answer. The magi brought valuable gifts, but that was not among them. This dark assertion will be illuminated later on.

Jim drew a package from his overcoat pocket and threw it upon the table.

"Don't make any mistake, Dell," he said, "about me. I don't think there's anything in the way of a haircut or a shave or a shampoo that could make me like my girl any less. But if you'll unwrap that package you may see why you had me going a while at first."

White fingers and nimble tore at the string and paper. And then an ecstatic scream of joy; and then, alas! a quick feminine change to hysterical tears and wails, necessitating the immediate employment of all the comforting powers of the lord of the flat.

For there lay The Combs—the set of combs, side and back, that Della had worshipped long in a Broadway window. Beautiful combs, pure tortoise shell, with jeweled rims—just the shade to wear in the beautiful vanished hair. They were expensive combs, she knew, and her heart had simply craved and yearned over them without the least hope of possession. And now, they were hers, but the tresses that should have adorned the coveted adornments were gone.

But she hugged them to her bosom, and at length she was able to look up with dim eyes and a smile and say: "My hair grows so fast, Jim!"

And then Della leaped up like a little singed cat and cried, "Oh, oh!"

Jim had not yet seen his beautiful present. She held it out to him eagerly upon her open palm. The dull precious metal seemed to flash with a reflection of her bright and ardent spirit.

"Isn't it a dandy, Jim? I hunted all over town to find it. You'll have to look at the time a hundred times a day now. Give me your watch. I want to see how it looks on it."

Instead of obeying, Jim tumbled down on the couch and put his hands under the back of his head and smiled. "Dell," said he, "let's put our Christmas presents away and keep 'em a while. They're too nice to use just at present. I sold the watch to get the money to buy your combs. And now suppose you put the chops on."

The magi, as you know, were wise men—wonderfully wise men—who brought gifts to the Babe in the manger. They invented the art of giving Christmas presents. Being wise, their gifts were no doubt wise ones, possibly bearing the privilege of exchange in case of duplication. And here I have lamely related to you the uneventful chronicle of two foolish children in a flat who most unwisely sacrificed for each other the greatest treasures of their house. But in a last word to the wise of these days let it be said that of all who give gifts these two were the wisest. O all who give and receive gifts, such as they are wisest. Everywhere they are wisest. They are the magi.

Review Questions
1. Why was Della upset?
2. What were the James Dillingham Youngs' two prized possessions?
3. What did Della want to buy for Jim? How did she get enough money?
4. What gift did Jim give Della? How did he get enough money?
5. What was the irony of Della's and Jim's gifts to each other?

Thought Questions
1. Have you ever given up something you loved for someone you cared about? Why did you do it? How did you feel afterward?
2. What does Christmas mean to you? Are gifts an important part? Why or why not?
3. Is self-sacrifice always a good thing? Explain.
4. Did Della and Jim give each other wise gifts? Did O. Henry think so? Why?
5. Why do you think O. Henry called this story "The Gift of the Magi"?

Reading Skills
VOCABULARY

These first seven reading assignments are a great opportunity to brush up on the reading skills mentioned in the introduction. For "The Gift of the Magi," practice dealing with unfamiliar vocabulary.

O. Henry is famous for using large or uncommon words in his stories. Here are a few words you may not have recognized. First, try to figure out what the words mean by looking at them in context in the story. Write down your tentative definition below. Now use a good dictionary to find a definition for each word and jot the definition in the margins of the story. Compare your guesses to the actual meaning of the word to see how close you were.

If you came across other words you didn't know, write them down below, and take a minute to look them up as well. The next time you read the story, mentally replace the difficult words with a synonym you do know, until the new words become a comfortable part of your vocabulary.

Vocabulary List

1. Imputation –

2. Parsimony –

3. Mendicancy –

4. Appertaining –

5. Depreciate –

6. Meretricious –

The Ransom of Red Chief
O. Henry

O. Henry's ability to create humor by placing very different characters side by side and giving each one a distinct voice is particularly evident in stories like "The Ransom of Red Chief," which was published in 1910 as a part of the collection *Whirligigs*. In addition, "The Ransom of Red Chief" provides another example of the surprise endings for which O. Henry became famous.

It looked like a good thing: but wait till I tell you. We were down South, in Alabama — Bill Driscoll and myself — when this kidnapping idea struck us. It was, as Bill afterward expressed it, "during a moment of temporary mental apparition"; but we didn't find that out till later.

There was a town down there, as flat as a flannel-cake, and called Summit, of course. It contained inhabitants of as undeleterious and self-satisfied a class of peasantry as ever clustered around a Maypole.

Bill and me had a joint capital of about six hundred dollars, and we needed just two thousand dollars more to pull off a fraudulent town-lot scheme in Western Illinois with. We talked it over on the front steps of the hotel. Philoprogenitiveness, says we, is strong in semi-rural communities; therefore and for other reasons, a kidnapping project ought to do better there than in the radius of newspapers that send reporters out in plain clothes to stir up talk about such things. We knew that Summit couldn't get after us with anything stronger than constables and maybe some lackadaisical bloodhounds and a diatribe or two in the Weekly Farmers' Budget. So, it looked good.

We selected for our victim the only child of a prominent citizen named Ebenezer Dorset. The father was respectable and tight, a mortgage fancier and a stern, upright collection-plate passer and forecloser. The kid was a boy of ten, with bas-relief freckles, and hair the colour of the cover of the magazine you buy at the news-stand when you want to catch a train. Bill and me figured that Ebenezer would melt down for a ransom of two thousand dollars to a cent. But wait till I tell you.

About two miles from Summit was a little mountain, covered with a dense cedar brake. On the rear elevation of this mountain was a cave. There we stored provisions. One evening after sundown, we drove in a buggy past old Dorset's house. The kid was in the street, throwing rocks at a kitten on the opposite fence.

"Hey, little boy!" says Bill, "would you like to have a bag of candy and a nice ride?"

The boy catches Bill neatly in the eye with a piece of brick.

"That will cost the old man an extra five hundred dollars," says Bill, climbing over the wheel.

That boy put up a fight like a welter-weight cinnamon bear; but, at last, we got him down in the bottom of the buggy and drove away. We took him up to the cave and I hitched the horse in the cedar brake. After dark I drove the buggy to the little village, three miles away, where we had hired it, and walked back to the mountain.

Bill was pasting court-plaster over the scratches and bruises on his features. There was a fire burning behind the big rock at the entrance of the cave, and the boy was watching a pot of boiling coffee, with two buzzard tailfeathers stuck in his red hair. He points a stick at me when I come up, and says:

"Ha! Cursed paleface, do you dare to enter the camp of Red Chief, the terror of the plains?"

"He's all right now," says Bill, rolling up his trousers and examining some bruises on his shins. "We're playing Indian. We're making Buffalo Bill's show look like magic-lantern views of Palestine in the town hall. I'm Old Hank, the Trapper, Red Chief's captive, and I'm to be scalped at daybreak. By Geronimo! that kid can kick hard."

Yes, sir, that boy seemed to be having the time of his life. The fun of camping out in a cave had made him forget that he was a captive, himself. He immediately christened me Snake-eye, the Spy, and announced that, when his braves returned from the warpath, I was to be broiled at the stake at the rising of the sun. Then we had supper; and he filled his mouth full of bacon and bread and gravy, and began to talk. He made a during-dinner speech something like this:

"I like this fine. I never camped out before; but I had a pet 'possum once, and I was nine last birthday. I hate to go to school. Rats ate up sixteen of Jimmy Talbot's aunt's speckled hen's eggs. Are there any real Indians in these woods? I want some more gravy. Does the trees moving make the wind blow? We had five puppies. What makes your nose so red, Hank? My father has lots of money. Are the stars hot? I whipped Ed Walker twice, Saturday. I don't like girls. You dassent catch toads unless with a string. Do oxen make any noise? Why are oranges round? Have you got beds to sleep on in this cave? Amos Murray has got six toes. A parrot can talk, but a monkey or a fish can't. How many does it take to make twelve?"

Every few minutes he would remember that he was a pesky redskin, and pick up his stick rifle and tiptoe to the mouth of the cave to rubber for the scouts of the hated paleface. Now and then he would let out a war-whoop that made Old Hank the Trapper shiver. That boy had Bill terrorized from the start.

"Red Chief," says I to the kid, "would you like to go home?"

"Aw, what for?" says he. "I don't have any fun at home. I hate to go to school. I like to camp out. You won't take me back home again, Snake-eye, will you?"

"Not right away," says I. "We'll stay here in the cave a while."

"All right!" says he. "That'll be fine. I never had such fun in all my life."

We went to bed about eleven o'clock. We spread down some wide blankets and quilts and put Red Chief between us. We weren't afraid he'd run away. He kept us awake for three hours, jumping up and reaching for his rifle and screeching: "Hist! pard," in mine and Bill's ears, as the fancied crackle of a twig or the rustle of a leaf revealed to his young imagination the stealthy approach of the outlaw band. At last, I fell into a troubled sleep, and dreamed that I had been kidnapped and chained to a tree by a ferocious pirate with red hair.

Just at daybreak, I was awakened by a series of awful screams from Bill. They weren't yells, or howls, or shouts, or whoops, or yalps, such as you'd expect from a manly set of vocal organs – they were simply indecent, terrifying, humiliating screams, such as women emit when they see ghosts or caterpillars. It's an awful thing to hear a strong, desperate, fat man scream incontinently in a cave at daybreak.

I jumped up to see what the matter was. Red Chief was sitting on Bill's chest, with one hand twined in Bill's hair. In the other he had the sharp case-knife we used for slicing bacon; and he was industriously and realistically trying to take Bill's scalp, according to the sentence that had been pronounced upon him the evening before.

I got the knife away from the kid and made him lie down again. But, from that moment, Bill's spirit was broken. He laid down on his side of the bed, but he never closed an eye again in sleep as long as that boy was with us. I dozed off for a while, but along toward sun-up I remembered that Red Chief had said I was to be burned at the stake at the rising of the sun. I wasn't nervous or afraid; but I sat up and lit my pipe and leaned against a rock.

"What you getting up so soon for, Sam?" asked Bill.

"Me?" says I. "Oh, I got a kind of a pain in my shoulder. I thought sitting up would rest it."

"You're a liar!" says Bill. "You're afraid. You was to be burned at sunrise, and you was afraid he'd do it. And he would, too, if he could find a match. Ain't it awful, Sam? Do you think anybody will pay out money to get a little imp like that back home?"

"Sure," said I. "A rowdy kid like that is just the kind that parents dote on. Now, you and the Chief get up and cook breakfast, while I go up on the top of this mountain and reconnoiter."

I went up on the peak of the little mountain and ran my eye over the contiguous vicinity. Over toward Summit I expected to see the sturdy yeomanry of the village armed with scythes and pitchforks beating the countryside for the dastardly kidnappers. But what I saw was a peaceful landscape dotted with one man ploughing with a dun mule. Nobody was dragging the creek; no couriers dashed hither and yon, bringing tidings of no news to the distracted parents. There was a sylvan attitude of somnolent sleepiness pervading that section of the external outward surface of Alabama that lay exposed to my view. "Perhaps," says I to myself, "it has not yet been discovered that the wolves have borne away the tender lambkin from the fold. Heaven help the wolves!" says I, and I went down the mountain to breakfast.

When I got to the cave I found Bill backed up against the side of it, breathing hard, and the boy threatening to smash him with a rock half as big as a cocoanut.

"He put a red-hot boiled potato down my back," explained Bill, "and then mashed it with his foot; and I boxed his ears. Have you got a gun about you, Sam?"

I took the rock away from the boy and kind of patched up the argument. "I'll fix you," says the kid to Bill. "No man ever yet struck the Red Chief but what he got paid for it. You better beware!"

After breakfast the kid takes a piece of leather with strings wrapped around it out of his pocket and goes outside the cave unwinding it.

"What's he up to now?" says Bill, anxiously. "You don't think he'll run away, do you, Sam?"

"No fear of it," says I. "He don't seem to be much of a home body. But we've got to fix up some plan about the ransom. There don't seem to be much excitement around Summit on account of his disappearance; but maybe they haven't realized yet that he's gone. His folks may think he's spending the night with Aunt Jane or one of the neighbours. Anyhow, he'll be missed to-day. To-night we must get a message to his father demanding the two thousand dollars for his return."

Just then we heard a kind of war-whoop, such as David might have emitted when he knocked out the champion Goliath. It was a sling that Red Chief had pulled out of his pocket, and he was whirling it around his head.

I dodged, and heard a heavy thud and a kind of a sigh from Bill, like a horse gives out when you take his saddle off. A niggerhead rock the size of an egg had caught Bill just behind his left ear. He loosened himself all over and fell in the fire across the frying pan of hot water for washing the dishes. I dragged him out and poured cold water on his head for half an hour.

By and by, Bill sits up and feels behind his ear and says: "Sam, do you know who my favourite Biblical character is?"

"Take it easy," says I. "You'll come to your senses presently."

"King Herod," says he. "You won't go away and leave me here alone, will you, Sam?"

I went out and caught that boy and shook him until his freckles rattled.

"If you don't behave," says I, "I'll take you straight home. Now, are you going to be good, or not?"

"I was only funning," says he sullenly. "I didn't mean to hurt Old Hank. But what did he hit me for? I'll behave, Snake-eye, if you won't send me home, and if you'll let me play the Black Scout to-day."

"I don't know the game," says I. "That's for you and Mr. Bill to decide. He's your playmate for the day. I'm going away for a while, on business. Now, you come in and make friends with him and say you are sorry for hurting him, or home you go, at once."

I made him and Bill shake hands, and then I took Bill aside and told him I was going to Poplar Cove, a little village three miles from the cave, and find out what I could about how the kidnapping had been regarded in Summit. Also, I thought it best to send a peremptory letter to old man Dorset that day, demanding the ransom and dictating how it should be paid.

"You know, Sam," says Bill, "I've stood by you without batting an eye in earthquakes, fire and flood – in poker games, dynamite outrages, police raids, train robberies and cyclones. I never lost my nerve yet till we kidnapped that two-legged skyrocket of a kid. He's got me going. You won't leave me long with him, will you, Sam?"

"I'll be back some time this afternoon," says I. "You must keep the boy amused and quiet till I return. And now we'll write the letter to old Dorset."

Bill and I got paper and pencil and worked on the letter while Red Chief, with a blanket wrapped around him, strutted up and down, guarding the mouth of the cave. Bill begged me tearfully to make the ransom fifteen hundred dollars instead of two thousand. "I ain't attempting," says he, "to decry the celebrated moral aspect of parental affection, but we're dealing with humans, and it ain't human for anybody to give up two thousand dollars for that forty-pound chunk of freckled wildcat. I'm willing to take a chance at fifteen hundred dollars. You can charge the difference up to me."

So, to relieve Bill, I acceded, and we collaborated a letter that ran this way:

Ebenezer Dorset, Esq.:

We have your boy concealed in a place far from Summit. It is useless for you or the most skilful detectives to attempt to find him. Absolutely, the only terms on which you can have him restored to you are these: We demand fifteen hundred dollars in large bills for his return; the money to be left at midnight to-night at the same spot and in the same box as your reply – as hereinafter described. If you agree to these terms, send your answer in writing by a solitary messenger to-night at half-past eight o'clock. After crossing Owl Creek, on the road to Poplar Cove, there are three large trees about a hundred yards apart, close to the fence of the wheat field on the right-hand side. At the bottom of the fence-post, opposite the third tree, will be found a small pasteboard box. The messenger will place the answer in this box and return immediately to Summit. If you attempt any treachery or fail to comply with our demand as stated, you will never see your boy again. If you pay the money as demanded, he will be returned to you safe and well within three hours. These terms are final, and if you do not accede to them no further communication will be attempted.

TWO DESPERATE MEN.

I addressed this letter to Dorset, and put it in my pocket. As I was about to start, the kid comes up to me and says:

"Aw, Snake-eye, you said I could play the Black Scout while you was gone."

"Play it, of course," says I. "Mr. Bill will play with you. What kind of a game is it?"

"I'm the Black Scout," says Red Chief, "and I have to ride to the stockade to warn the settlers that the Indians are coming. I'm tired of playing Indian myself. I want to be the Black Scout."

"All right," says I. "It sounds harmless to me. I guess Mr. Bill will help you foil the pesky savages."

"What am I to do?" asks Bill, looking at the kid suspiciously.

"You are the hoss," says Black Scout. "Get down on your hands and knees. How can I ride to the stockade without a hoss?"

"You'd better keep him interested," said I, "till we get the scheme going. Loosen up."

Bill gets down on his all fours, and a look comes in his eye like a rabbit's when you catch it in a trap.

"How far is it to the stockade, kid?" he asks, in a husky manner of voice.

"Ninety miles," says the Black Scout. "And you have to hump yourself to get there on time. Whoa, now!"

"For Heaven's sake," says Bill, "hurry back, Sam, as soon as you can. I wish we hadn't made the ransom more than a thousand. Say, you quit kicking me or I'll get up and warm you good."

I walked over to Poplar Cove and sat around the post-office and store, talking with the chawbacons that came in to trade. One whiskerando says that he hears Summit is all upset on account of Elder Ebenezer Dorset's boy having been lost or stolen. That was all I wanted to know. I bought some smoking tobacco, referred casually to the price of black-eyed peas, posted my letter surreptitiously and came away. The postmaster said the mail-carrier would come by in an hour to take the mail on to Summit.

When I got back to the cave Bill and the boy were not to be found. I explored the vicinity of the cave, and risked a yodel or two, but there was no response.

So I lighted my pipe and sat down on a mossy bank to await developments.

In about half an hour I heard the bushes rustle, and Bill wabbled out into the little glade in front of the cave. Behind him was the kid, stepping softly like a scout, with a broad grin on his face. Bill stopped, took off his hat and wiped his face with a red handkerchief. The kid stopped about eight feet behind him.

"Sam," says Bill, "I suppose you'll think I'm a renegade, but I couldn't help it. I'm a grown person with masculine proclivities and habits of self-defense, but there is a time when all systems of egotism and predominance fail. The boy is gone. I have sent him home. All is off. There was martyrs in old times," goes on Bill, "that suffered death rather than give up the particular graft they enjoyed. None of 'em ever was subjugated to such supernatural tortures as I have been. I tried to be faithful to our articles of depredation; but there came a limit."

"What's the trouble, Bill?" I asks him.

"I was rode," says Bill, "the ninety miles to the stockade, not barring an inch. Then, when the settlers was rescued, I was given oats. Sand ain't a palatable substitute. And then, for an hour I had to try to explain to him why there was nothin' in holes, how a road can run both ways and what makes the grass green. I tell you, Sam, a human can only stand so much. I takes him by the neck of his clothes and drags him down the mountain. On the way he kicks my legs black-and-blue from the knees down; and I've got to have two or three bites on my thumb and hand cauterized."

"But he's gone" – continues Bill – "gone home. I showed him the road to Summit and kicked him about eight feet nearer there at one kick. I'm sorry we lose the ransom; but it was either that or Bill Driscoll to the madhouse."

Bill is puffing and blowing, but there is a look of ineffable peace and growing content on his rose-pink features.

"Bill," says I, "there isn't any heart disease in your family, is there?"

"No," says Bill, "nothing chronic except malaria and accidents. Why?"

"Then you might turn around," says I, "and have a look behind you."

Bill turns and sees the boy, and loses his complexion and sits down plump on the ground and begins to pluck aimlessly at grass and little sticks. For an hour I was afraid for his mind. And then I told him that my scheme was to put the whole job through immediately and that we would get the ransom and be off with it by midnight if old Dorset fell in with our proposition. So Bill braced up enough to give the kid a weak sort of a smile and a promise to play the Russian in a Japanese war with him as soon as he felt a little better.

I had a scheme for collecting that ransom without danger of being caught by counterplots that ought to commend itself to professional kidnappers. The tree under which the answer was to be left – and the money later on – was close to the road fence with big, bare fields on all sides. If a gang of constables should be watching for any one to come for the note they could see him a long way off crossing the fields or in the road. But no, sirree! At half-past eight I was up in that tree as well hidden as a tree toad, waiting for the messenger to arrive.

Exactly on time, a half-grown boy rides up the road on a bicycle, locates the pasteboard box at the foot of the fence-post, slips a folded piece of paper into it and pedals away again back toward Summit.

I waited an hour and then concluded the thing was square. I slid down the tree, got the note, slipped along the fence till I struck the woods, and was back at the cave in another half an hour. I opened the note, got near the lantern and read it to Bill. It was written with a pen in a crabbed hand, and the sum and substance of it was this:

Two Desperate Men.

Gentlemen: I received your letter to-day by post, in regard to the ransom you ask for the return of my son. I think you are a little high in your demands, and I hereby make you a counter-proposition, which I am inclined to believe you will accept. You bring Johnny home and pay me two hundred and fifty dollars in cash, and I agree to take him off your hands. You had better come at night, for the neighbours believe he is lost, and I couldn't be responsible for what they would do to anybody they saw bringing him back.

Very respectfully,
EBENEZER DORSET.

"Great pirates of Penzance!" says I; "of all the impudent –"

But I glanced at Bill, and hesitated. He had the most appealing look in his eyes I ever saw on the face of a dumb or a talking brute.

"Sam," says he, "what's two hundred and fifty dollars, after all? We've got the money. One more night of this kid will send me to a bed in Bedlam. Besides being a thorough gentleman, I think Mr. Dorset is a spendthrift for making us such a liberal offer. You ain't going to let the chance go, are you?"

"Tell you the truth, Bill," says I, "this little he ewe lamb has somewhat got on my nerves too. We'll take him home, pay the ransom and make our get-away."

We took him home that night. We got him to go by telling him that his father had bought a silver-mounted rifle and a pair of moccasins for him, and we were going to hunt bears the next day.

It was just twelve o'clock when we knocked at Ebenezer's front door. Just at the moment when I should have been abstracting the fifteen hundred dollars from the box under the tree, according to the original proposition, Bill was counting out two hundred and fifty dollars into Dorset's hand.

When the kid found out we were going to leave him at home he started up a howl like a calliope and fastened himself as tight as a leech to Bill's leg. His father peeled him away gradually, like a porous plaster.

"How long can you hold him?" asks Bill.

"I'm not as strong as I used to be," says old Dorset, "but I think I can promise you ten minutes."

"Enough," says Bill. "In ten minutes I shall cross the Central, Southern and Middle Western States, and be legging it trippingly for the Canadian border."

And, as dark as it was, and as fat as Bill was, and as good a runner as I am, he was a good mile and a half out of Summit before I could catch up with him.

Review Questions
1. What was Sam and Bill's scheme for making money?
2. What was the boy doing to Bill when Sam woke up?
3. Why did Bill say King Herod was his favorite Biblical character?
4. Why did Sam ask Bill if there was heart disease in his family?
5. What was Ebenezer Dorset's counter-proposal?

Thought Questions
1. Does it seem unusual that a common kidnapper would speak the way Sam spoke? Explain.
2. When do you think Bill and Sam's scheme went wrong?
3. Bill was much larger and stronger than Red Chief. Why was he so afraid of the boy?
4. Do you think Ebenezer Dorset loved his son? Why or why not?
5. Is there a moral to O. Henry's story? If so, what is it?

Reading Skills
VOCABULARY

"The Ransom of Red Chief" gives you another opportunity to practice dealing with unfamiliar vocabulary. Here are a few words you may not have recognized. As you did with "The Gift of the Magi," first try to figure out what the words mean by looking at them in context in the story. Write down your tentative definition below. Then use a good dictionary to find a definition for each word and jot the definition in the margins of the story. Pay attention to instances in which O. Henry creates words by altering existing ones (see #2 below).

1. Apparition –

2. Undeleterious (*hint, see deleterious*) –

3. Philoprogenitive –

4. Diatribe –

5. Bas-relief –

6. Reconnoiter –

7. Proclivities –

"If"

Rudyard Kipling

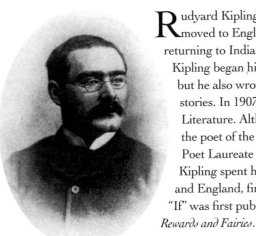

Rudyard Kipling (1865-1936) was born in India but moved to England to complete his education before returning to India to work in the newspaper business. Kipling began his literary career writing short stories, but he also wrote volumes of poetry and children's stories. In 1907, Kipling received the Nobel Prize in Literature. Although Kipling was widely regarded as the poet of the British Empire, he declined the post of Poet Laureate when it was offered. A frequent traveler, Kipling spent his later years between the United States and England, finally settling in England. The poem "If" was first published in 1910 as part of the collection *Rewards and Fairies*.

If you can keep your head when all about you
Are losing theirs and blaming it on you;
If you can trust yourself when all men doubt you,
But make allowance for their doubting too;
If you can wait and not be tired by waiting,
Or being lied about, don't deal in lies,
Or being hated, don't give way to hating,
And yet don't look too good, nor talk too wise:

If you can dream—and not make dreams your master;
If you can think—and not make thoughts your aim;
If you can meet with Triumph and Disaster
And treat those two impostors just the same;
If you can bear to hear the truth you've spoken
Twisted by knaves to make a trap for fools,
Or watch the things you gave your life to, broken,
And stoop and build 'em up with worn-out tools:

If you can make one heap of all your winnings
And risk it on one turn of pitch-and-toss,
And lose, and start again at your beginnings
And never breathe a word about your loss;
If you can force your heart and nerve and sinew
To serve your turn long after they are gone,
And so hold on when there is nothing in you
Except the Will which says to them: "Hold on!"

If you can talk with crowds and keep your virtue,
Or walk with Kings—nor lose the common touch,
If neither foes nor loving friends can hurt you,
If all men count with you, but none too much;
If you can fill the unforgiving minute
With sixty seconds' worth of distance run,
Yours is the Earth and everything that's in it,
And—which is more—you'll be a Man, my son!

Review Questions
1. What two situations does Kipling call "those two imposters"?
2. What image does Kipling use in the third stanza to make his point about taking risks?
3. What reward does Kipling say will belong to those who fulfill his "If" statements?

Thought Questions
1. What values of manhood does Kipling's poem promote?
2. What does it mean to "make allowance for [other men's] doubting"?
3. Why do you think Kipling calls Triumph and Disaster imposters? Do you agree?
4. In what situations is it challenging to "talk with crowds and keep your virtue"? Why might public attention threaten virtue?

Reading Practice
THEMES

Kipling's "If" is not a long poem, but it lays out a comprehensive picture of what it means to be a man. The poem is organized as a series of propositions ("If you can _____"), and the reward or payoff is only mentioned in the final two lines.

Because this is poetry, as you read and re-read the poem, think carefully about the language and images that Kipling uses to make his point. Pay particular attention to the connecting words of the poem (conjunctions like *and, or,* and *but*). What effect does the poem's structure produce?

Finally, ask yourself what similarities, both in form and content, you see in Kipling's characteristics of manhood. What kind of examples does he use to make his point? Try to identify the themes of the poem and its picture of a true man.

"If, for Girls"
J. P. McEvoy

Joseph Patrick McEvoy (1897-1958) was born in New York, where he went on to become a writer for many different forms of media. Over the course of his career, in addition to writing poetry and greeting card jingles, McEvoy also wrote for a popular comic strip and worked in film and theater. His original screenplays and film adaptations featured actors and actresses like Shirley Temple and Cary Grant. McEvoy's poem "If, for Girls," which is an adaptation of Kipling's poem "If," was published in 1924.

If you can hear the whispering about you,
And never yield to deal in whispers, too;
If you can bravely smile when loved ones doubt you
And never doubt, in turn, what loved ones do;
If you can keep a sweet and gentle spirit
In spite of fame or fortune, rank or place,
And though you win your goal or only near it,
Can win with poise or lose with equal grace;

If you can meet with Unbelief, believing,
And hallow in your heart a simple Creed;
If you can meet Deception, undeceiving,
And learn to look to God for all you need;
If you can be what girls should be to mothers:
Chums in joy and comrades in distress,
And be unto others as you'd have the others
Be unto you—no more, and yet no less;

If you can keep within your heart the power
To say that firm, unconquerable "No";
If you can brave a present shadowed hour,
Rather than yield to build a future woe;
If you can love, yet not let loving master,
But keep yourself within your own self's clasp,
And let not Dreaming lead you to disaster,
Nor Pity's fascination loose your grasp;

If you can lock your heart on confidences,
Nor ever needlessly in turn confide;
If you can put behind you all pretenses
Of mock humility or foolish pride;
If you can keep the simple, homely virtue
Of walking right with God—then have no fear
That anything in all the world can hurt you—
And—which is more—you'll be a Woman, dear.

Review Questions
1. What, according to McEvoy, should girls be to mothers?
2. What "simple, homely virtue" does McEvoy recommend?
3. What reward does McEvoy say will belong to those who fulfill his "If" statements?

Thought Questions
1. What values of womanhood does McEvoy's poem promote?
2. This is a poem about womanhood, but it was written by a man. Do you think it would have been different if a woman had written it? If so, how?
3. What does it mean to "needlessly in turn confide"? Why might it be a bad thing?
4. Why do you think McEvoy chose to re-write Kipling's poem for girls? How do you think McEvoy's vision of womanhood compares to Kipling's view of manhood?

Reading Practice
QUOTES

When you write about or discuss the book, you will need evidence, and it is much easier to mark quotes as you go than to relocate specific passages when you need them. This poem is short but to the point. Imagine that you were going to write an essay about this poem. Try to pick out one or two especially strong phrases you might want to quote in full.

Now take a minute to think about how you could paraphrase, or put in your own words, the contents of this poem. Without looking at the original, try to use no more than four sentences (one per stanza) to summarize the message of the poem. Make sure the word choice and the sentence structure are your own. Now do the same thing in only one sentence. Think about eliminating detail and selecting only the most important pieces.

It is important to be able to choose when to quote and when to paraphrase. Ask yourself why you chose to quote some lines and paraphrase others. When an author uses a phrase in a very specific way or words an idea in a unique way, you may want to quote the words exactly. In contrast, if you want to convey the general idea of a piece, you might paraphrase. As you read, think about what makes a sentence or phrase worth quoting, and why other statements are easier to paraphrase.

"A Model of Christian Charity" (excerpt)
John Winthrop

John Winthrop (1588-1649) was a prominent leader in early America. Winthrop was born in England, but when Charles I became king, Winthrop, a Puritan, recognized that his beliefs were at odds with the king's Roman Catholic sympathies. In 1629, Winthrop joined a group of merchants, also Puritans, seeking permission from the king to travel to the New World and establish the Massachusetts Bay colony. When their petition was approved, Winthrop was chosen to be the colony's first governor. He delivered the sermon "A Model of Christian Charity" in 1630, probably while on board the ship *Arbella* on the way to America. This selection is an excerpt from that sermon.

God Almighty in His most holy and wise providence hath so disposed of the condition of mankind, as in all times some must be rich, some poor, some high and eminent in power and dignity; others mean and in subjection.

The Reason hereof: First, to hold conformity with the rest of His world, being delighted to show forth the glory of His wisdom in the variety and differences of the creatures and the glory of His power, in ordering all these differences for the preservation and good of the whole, and the glory of His greatness, that as it is the glory of princes to have many officers, so this great King will have many stewards, counting Himself more honored in dispensing His gifts to man by man, than if He did it by His own immediate hands.

Secondly, that He might have the more occasion to manifest the work of His Spirit: first, upon the wicked in moderating and restraining them, so that the rich and mighty should not eat up the poor, nor the poor and despised rise up against their superiors and shake off their yoke. Secondly, in the regenerate, in exercising His graces in them, as in the great ones, their love, mercy, gentleness, temperance, etc., in the poor and inferior sort, their faith, patience, obedience, etc.

Thirdly, that every man might have need of others, and from hence they might be all knit more nearly together in the bonds of brotherly affection. From hence it appears plainly that no man is made more honorable than another or more wealthy etc., out of any particular and singular respect to himself, but for the glory of his Creator and the common good of the creature, man. Therefore God still reserves the property of these gifts to himself, as Ezekiel 16:17, He calls wealth "His gold and His silver"; and Proverbs 3:9, He claims their service as his due: "Honor the Lord with thy riches," etc. All men being thus (by divine providence) ranked into two sorts, rich and poor; under the first, are comprehended all such as are able to live comfortably by their own means duly improved; and all others are poor according to the former distribution. There are two rules whereby we are to walk one towards another: justice and mercy. These are always distinguished in their act and in their object, yet may they both concur in the same subject in each respect; as sometimes there may be an occasion of showing mercy to a rich man in some sudden danger of distress, and also doing of mere justice to a poor man in regard of some particular contract, etc. There is likewise a double law by which we are regulated in our conversation towards another. In both the former respects, the law of nature and the law of grace, or the moral law or the law of the gospel, to omit the rule of justice as not properly belonging to this purpose otherwise than it may fall into consideration in some particular cases. By the first of these laws, man as he was enabled so withal is commanded to love his neighbor as himself. Upon this ground stands all the precepts of the moral law, which concerns our dealings with men. To apply this to the works of mercy, this law requires two things: first, that every man afford his help to another in every want or distress; secondly, that he perform this out of the same affection, which makes him careful of his own good according to that of our Savior. "Whatsoever ye would that men should do to you." This was practiced by Abraham and Lot in entertaining the Angels and the old man of Gibea.

The law of grace or the gospel hath some difference from the former as in these respects: first, the law of nature was given to man in the estate of innocence; this of the gospel in the estate of regeneracy. Secondly, the former propounds one man to another, as the same flesh and image of God; this as a brother in Christ also, and in the communion of the same Spirit and so teacheth to put a difference between Christians and others. "Do good to all especially to the household of faith." Upon this ground the Israelites were to put a difference between the brethren of such as were strangers though not of the Canaanites. Thirdly, the law of nature could give no rules for dealing with enemies, for all to be considered as friends in the estate of innocence, but the gospel commands love to an enemy. Proof: "If thine enemy hungers, feed him; love your enemies, do good to them that hate you."

This law of the gospel propounds likewise a difference of seasons and occasions. There is a time when a Christian must sell all and give to the poor as they did in the Apostles' times. There is a time also when a Christian — though they give not all yet — must give beyond their ability, as they of Macedonia (2 Cor. 8:8). Likewise, community of perils calls for extraordinary liberality, and so doth the community in some special service for the church. Lastly, when there is no other means whereby our Christian brother may be relieved in his distress, we must help him beyond our ability, rather than tempt God in putting him upon help by miraculous or extraordinary means.

This duty of mercy is exercised in the kinds: giving, lending, and forgiving.

What rule shall a man observe in giving in respect of the measure? If the time and occasion be ordinary, he is to give out of his abundance — let him lay aside as God hath blessed him. If the time and occasion be extraordinary, he must be ruled by them; taking this withal, that then a man cannot likely do too much, especially if he may leave himself and his family under probable means of comfortable subsistence.

Some though, may object, "A man must lay up for posterity, the fathers lay up for posterity and children and he is worse than an infidel that provideth not for his own." For the first, it is plain that it is being spoken by way of comparison; it must be meant of the ordinary and usual course of fathers, and cannot extend to times and occasions extraordinary. For the other place, the Apostle speaks against such as walked inordinately, and it is without question, that he is worse than an infidel who through his own sloth and voluptuousness shall neglect to provide for his family.

Another may object: "The wise man's eyes are in his head and forseeth the plague"; therefore he must forecast and lay up against evil times when he or his may stand in need of all he can gather. Yet, this very argument Solomon useth to persuade to liberality: "Cast they bread upon the waters, for thou knowest not what evil may come upon the land." (Eccl. 11) " Make you friends of the riches of iniquity…" (Luke 16:9). You will ask how this shall be? Very well. For first, "He that gives to the poor lends to the Lord," and He will repay him even in this life an hundredfold to him or his. "The righteous is ever merciful and lendeth; and his seed enjoyeth the blessing"; and besides we know what advantage it will be to us in the day of account when many such witnesses shall stand forth for us to witness the improvement of our talent. And I would know of those who plead so much for laying up for time to come, whether they hold that to be. Matthew 6:19, "Lay not up for yourselves Treasures upon Earth." If they acknowledge it, what extent will they allow it? If only to those primitive times, let them consider the reason whereupon our Saviour grounds it: the first is that they are subject to the moth, the rust, the thief; secondly, they will steal away the heart, "where the treasure is, there will the heart be also." The reasons are of like force at all times; therefore, the exhortation must be general and perpetual with always in respect of the love and affection to riches and in regard of the things themselves when any special service for the church or particular distress of our brother do call for the use of them; otherwise it is not only lawful but necessary to lay up as Joseph did to have ready upon such occasions, as the Lord—whose stewards we are of them—shall call for them from us. Christ gives us an instance of the first, when He sent His disciples for the ass, and bids them answer the owner thus, "The Lord hath need of him"; so when the Tabernacle was to be built He sends to his people to call for their silver and gold, and yields them no other reason but that it was for His work. When Elisha comes to the widow of Sareptah and finds her preparing to make ready her pittance for herself and family, he bids her first provide for him. He challengeth first God's part, which she must give before she can serve her own family. All these teach us that the Lord looks that when He is pleased to call for His right in any thing we have, our own interest we have must stand aside, till His turn be served. For the other, we need look no further than that of 1 John 3:17, "He who hath this world's goods and seeth his brother to need, and shuts up his compassion from him, how dwelleth the love of God in him?", which comes punctually to this conclusion: "If thy brother be in want and thou canst help him, thou needst not make doubt of what thou shouldst do; if thou lovest God, thou must help him."

What rule must we observe in lending? Thou must observe whether thy brother hath present or probable or possible means of repaying thee. If there be none of those, thou must give him according it his necessity, rather than lend him as he requires. If he hath present means of repaying thee, thou are to look at him not as an act of mercy, but by way of commerce, wherein thou art to walk by the rule of justice; but, if his means of repaying thee be only probable or possible, then he is an object of thy mercy, thou must lend him, though there be danger of losing it. (Deut. 15:7-8) "If any of thy brethren be poor…thou shalt lend him sufficient." That men might not shift off this duty by the apparent hazard, He tells them that though the Year of Jubilee were at hand—when he must remit it, if he were not able to repay it before—yet he must lend him and that cheerfully. "It may not grieve thee to give him," saith He, and because some might object, "Why so I should soon impoverish myself and my family," he adds with all thy work, etc., for our Savior said (Matt. 5:42), "From him that would borrow of thee turn not away."

What rule must we observe in forgiving (a debt)? Whether thou didst lend by way of commerce or in mercy, if he hath nothing to pay thee, thou must forgive—except in cause where thou hast a surety or a lawful pledge. Deut. 15:1-2—Every seventh year the creditor was to quit that which he lent to his brother if he were poor as appears in verse 4. "Save when there shall be no poor with thee." In all these and like cases Christ was a general rule. (Matt. 7:22), "Whatsoever ye would that men should do to you, do ye the same to them also."

What rule must we observe and walk by in cause of community of peril? The same as before, but with more enlargement towards others and less respect towards ourselves, and our own right. Hence it was that in the primitive Church, they sold all, had all things in common, neither did any man say that which he possessed was his own. Likewise, in their return out of the captivity, because the work was great for the restoring of the church and the danger of enemies was common to all, Nehemiah directs the Jews to liberality and readiness in remitting their debts to their brethren, and disposing liberally to such as wanted, and stand not upon their own dues, which they might have demanded of them. Thus did some of our forefathers in times of persecution in England, and so did many of the faithful in other churches, whereof we keep an honorable remembrance of them; and it is to be observed that both in Scriptures and latter stories of the churches that such as have been most bountiful to the poor saints, especially in these extraordinary times and occasions, God hath left them highly commended to posterity, and as Zacheus, Cornelius, Dorcas, Bishop Hooper, the Cuttler of Brussells and divers others. Observe again that the Scripture gives no caution to restrain any from being over liberal this way; but all men to the liberal and cheerful practice hereof by the sweeter promises; as to instance one for many, Isaiah 58:6-9. "Is not this the fast that I have chosen to loose the bonds of wickedness, to take off the heavy burdens, to let the oppressed go free and to break every yoke…to deal thy bread to the hungry and to bring the poor that wander in to thy house, when thou seest the naked to cover them… and then, shall the light break forth as the morning, and thy health shall grow speedily, thy righteousness shall go before thee, God, and the glory of the Lord shall embrace thee; then thou shalt call and the Lord shall answer thee," etc. And from Isaiah 58:10, "If thou pour out thy soul to the hungry, then shall thy light spring out in darkness, and the Lord shall guide thee continually, and satisfy thy soul in draught, and make fat thy bones; thou shalt be like a watered garden…and they shalt be of thee that shall build the old waste places." On the contrary most heavy curses are laid upon such as are straightened towards the Lord and his people (Judges 5:23), "Curse ye Meroshe…because they came not to help the Lord." He who shutteth his ears from hearing the cry of the poor, he shall cry and shall not be heard: (Matt. 25) "Go ye cursed into everlasting fire," etc. "I was hungry and ye fed me not." (2 Cor. 9:6) "He that soweth sparingly shall reap sparingly."

The end is to improve our lives to do more service to the Lord; the comfort and increase of the body of Christ, whereof we are members; that ourselves and posterity may be the better preserved from the common corruptions of this evil world, to serve the Lord and work out our salvation under the power and purity of His holy ordinances.

Now the only way to avoid this shipwreck, and to provide for our posterity, is to follow the counsel of Micah, "to do justly, to love mercy, to walk humbly with our God." For this end we must be knit together, in this work, as one man, we must entertain each other in brotherly affection. We must be willing to abridge ourselves of our superfluities, for the supply of others' necessities. We must uphold a familiar commerce together in all meekness, gentleness, patience, and liberality. We must delight in each other; make others' conditions our own; rejoice together, mourn together, labor and suffer together, always having before our eyes our commission and community in the work, as members of the same body. So shall we "keep the unity of the Spirit in the bond of peace." The Lord will be our God and delight to dwell among us, as His own people, and will command a blessing upon us in all our ways, so that we shall see much more of his wisdom, power, goodness and truth, than formerly we have been acquainted with. We shall find that the God of Israel is among us, when ten of us shall be able to resist a thousand of our enemies; when He shall make us a praise and glory that men shall say of succeeding plantations, "the Lord make it like that of New England." For we must consider that we shall be as a city upon a hill. The eyes of all people are upon us. So that if we shall deal falsely with our God in this work we have undertaken, and so cause Him to withdraw His present help from us, we shall be made a story and a by-word through the world. We shall open the mouths of enemies to speak evil of the ways of God, and all professors for God's sake. We shall shame the faces of many of God's worthy servants, and cause their prayers to be turned into curses upon us till we be consumed out of the good land whither we are going.

(Deut. 30) "Beloved there is now set before us life and good, death and evil," in that we are commanded this day to love the Lord our God, and to love one another, to walk in His ways and to keep His commandments and His ordinance and His laws, and the articles of our covenant with Him that we may live and be multiplied, and that the Lord our God may bless us in the land whither we go to possess it. But if our hearts shall turn away, so that we will not obey, but shall be seduced, and worship and serve other gods, our pleasures and profits, and serve them; it is propounded unto us this day, "we shall surely perish out of the good land whither we pass over this vast sea to possess it."

Therefore let us choose life, that we and our seed may live, by obeying His voice and cleaving to Him, for He is our life, and our prosperity.

Review Questions

1. Why does Winthrop say some must be rich and some poor?
2. What two rules govern our interactions?
3. How do the laws of grace and nature differ?
4. What is the rule in lending, according to Winthrop?
5. How should we best provide for our posterity?

Thought Questions

1. Why do you think some people are rich and some are poor? Do you agree with Winthrop?
2. Do you think people should provide first for their families or for the poor? Explain.
3. What is a Year of Jubilee? Does it sound like a good idea?
4. Why did Winthrop call America a "City on a Hill"? Does it still fill that role?
5. Of what was Winthrop mainly trying to convince his listeners? Does he convince you?

Reading Skills
PLOT

Think about this sermon as a type of persuasive essay. The "plot" in this case is very similar to the kind of argument you will be trying to develop in your own writing. Look back over the sermon, and if you can, create an outline of Winthrop's main points. Pay attention to the transitions and "big moments," or turning points, of the sermon.

Take a look at the following paragraph:

> What rule must we observe in forgiving (a debt)? Whether thou didst lend by way of commerce or in mercy, if he hath nothing to pay thee, thou must forgive—except in cause where thou hast a surety or a lawful pledge. Deut. 15:1-2—Every seventh year the creditor was to quit that which he lent to his brother if he were poor as appears in verse 4. "Save when there shall be no poor with thee." In these and like cases Christ was a general rule. (Matt. 7:22), "Whatsoever ye would that men should do to you, do ye the same to them also."

Think about this passage as a mini-essay. Identify the question it asks (Winthrop's writing style makes it obvious in this case), the answer—or claim—Winthrop gives, the type of evidence he uses, and the way he incorporates that evidence into the paragraph.

Essays to Do Good (excerpt)
Cotton Mather

Cotton Mather (1663-1728) was born in America, and he followed his father's footsteps to become an ordained Congregational minister of the Second Church of Boston. Mather was a historian as well as a theologian, and his *Magnalia Christi Americana* provides an extensive record of the Christian history of the early colonies. Mather also wrote conduct books, including *Bonifacius*, or *Essays to Do Good*, which was published in 1710. This essay, "Much Occasion for Doing Good," is an excerpt from that larger work. (This version of the text is from an 1824 edition edited by George Burder.)

"Much Occasion for Doing Good"

Such glorious things are spoken in the oracles of God, concerning them who devise good, that a book of good devices may reasonably demand attention and acceptance from those who have any impressions of the most reasonable religion upon them. I am devising such a book; but at the same time offering a sorrowful demonstration, that if men would set themselves to devise good, a world of good might be done more than is now done in this "present evil world."

Much is requisite to be done that the great God and his Christ may be more known and served in the world; and that the errors which prevent men from glorifying their Creator and Redeemer may be rectified. Much is necessary to be done that the evil manners of the world, by which men are drowned in perdition, may be reformed; and mankind rescued from the epidemical corruption which has overwhelmed it. Much must be done that the miseries of the world may have suitable remedies provided for them; and that the wretched may be relieved and comforted.

The world contains, it is supposed, about a thousand millions of inhabitants. What an ample field do these afford, for doing good! In a word, the kingdom of God in the world calls for innumerable services from us. To do such things is to do good. Those men devise good, who form plans which have such a tendency, whether the objects be of a temporal or spiritual nature.

You see the general matter, appearing as yet but a chaos, which is to be wrought upon. O! that the good Spirit of God may now fall upon us, and carry on the glorious work which lies before us!

Review Questions
1. Why does Mather think Christians will read his book?
2. What is the purpose of doing good deeds?
3. "To do good," according to Mather, is to do what?

Thought Questions
1. Are good works what the world needs? If not, what does it need?
2. What do you think it means to "do good"? What is the hardest part of doing good things?
3. If someone does good for selfish motives, does that make his/her deeds less good? Explain.

Reading Skills
QUOTES

The selection from this sermon is short but to the point. Imagine that you were going to write an essay about Mather based on this selection. Try to pick out one or two especially strong phrases or quotes that you might use when writing about this sermon.

In contrast, what points from the piece would you choose to paraphrase? Pick one or two, and without looking at the original, write a sentence summarizing each point. Make sure the word choice and the sentence structure of each paraphrase is your own.

Finally, ask yourself why you chose to quote some lines and paraphrase others. Think about what makes a sentence or phrase worth quoting, and why other statements are easier to paraphrase.

"The Method of Grace"
George Whitefield

George Whitefield (1714-1770) was ordained as a priest in the Church of England while still in his early twenties. He later became a leader of the Methodist movement in England, and he was closely associated with other church reformers including John and Charles Wesley. He was a prolific speaker, and he visited America a number of times during his years of ministry, where he played an important role in the Great Awakening. "The Method of Grace" is the common name of his Sermon 58, part of his collected sermons, which were first published in 1771-1772.

"The Method of Grace"

Jeremiah 6:14, "They have healed also the hurt of the daughter of my people slightly, saying, Peace, peace, when there is no peace."

As God can send a nation or people no greater blessing than to give them faithful, sincere, and upright ministers, so the greatest curse that God can possibly send upon a people in this world, is to give them over to blind, unregenerate, carnal, lukewarm, and unskilled guides. And yet, in all ages, we find that there have been many wolves in sheep's clothing, many that daubed with untempered mortar, that prophesied smoother things than God did allow. As it was formerly, so it is now; there are many that corrupt the Word of God and deal deceitfully with it. It was so in a special manner in the prophet Jeremiah's time; and he, faithful to his Lord, faithful to that God who employed him, did not fail from time to time to open his mouth against them, and to bear a noble testimony to the honor of that God in whose name he from time to time spake. If you will read this prophecy, you will find that none spake more against such ministers than Jeremiah, and here especially in the chapter out of which the text is taken, he speaks very severely against them – he charges them with several crimes;

particularly, he charges them with covetousness: "For," says he in the 13th verse, "from the least of them even to the greatest of them, every one is given to covetousness; and from the prophet even unto the priest, every one dealeth false." And then, in the words of the text, in a more special manner, he exemplifies how they had dealt falsely, how they had behaved treacherously to poor souls: says he, "They have healed also the hurt of the daughter of my people slightly, saying, Peace, peace, when there is no peace." The prophet, in the name of God, had been denouncing war against the people, he had been telling them that their house should be left desolate, and that the Lord would certainly visit the land with war. "Therefore," says he, in the 11th verse, "I am full of the fury of the Lord; I am weary with holding in; I will pour it out upon the children abroad, and upon the assembly of young men together; for even the husband with the wife shall be taken, the aged with him that is full of days. And their houses shall be turned unto others, with their fields and wives together; for I will stretch out my hand upon the inhabitants of the land, saith the Lord."

The prophet gives a thundering message, that they might be terrified and have some convictions and inclinations to repent; but it seems that the false prophets, the false priests, went about stifling people's convictions, and when they were hurt or a little terrified, they were for daubing over the wound, telling them that Jeremiah was but an enthusiastic preacher, that there could be no such thing as war among them, and saying to people, Peace, peace, be still, when the prophet told them there was no peace. The words, then, refer primarily unto outward things, but I verily believe have also a further reference to the soul, and are to be referred to those false teachers, who, when people were under conviction of sin, when people were beginning to look towards heaven, were for stifling their convictions and telling them they were good enough before. And, indeed, people generally love to have it so; our hearts are exceedingly deceitful, and desperately wicked; none but the eternal God knows how treacherous they are. How many of us cry, Peace, peace, to our souls, when there is no peace! How many are there who are now settled upon their lees, that now think they are Christians, that now flatter themselves that they have an interest in Jesus Christ; whereas if we come to examine their experiences, we shall find that their peace is but a peace of the devil's making – it is not a peace of God's giving – it is not a peace that passeth human understanding. It is matter, therefore, of great importance, my dear hearers, to know whether we may speak peace to our hearts. We are all desirous of peace; peace is an unspeakable blessing; how can we live without peace? And, therefore, people from time to time must be taught how far they must go, and what must be wrought in them, before they can speak peace to their hearts. This is what I design at present, that I may deliver my soul, that I may be free from the blood of those to whom I preach – that I may not fail to declare the whole counsel of God. I shall, from the words of the text, endeavor to show you what you must undergo, and what must be wrought in you before you can speak peace to your hearts.

But before I come directly to this, give me leave to premise a caution or two. And the first is, that I take it for granted you believe religion to be an inward thing; you believe it to be a work in the heart, a work wrought in the soul by the power of the Spirit of God. If you do not believe this, you do not believe your Bibles. If you do not believe this, though you have got your Bibles in your hand, you hate the Lord Jesus Christ in your heart; for religion is everywhere represented in Scripture as the work of God in the heart. "The kingdom of God is within us," says our Lord; and, "He is not a Christian who is one outwardly; but he is a Christian who is one inwardly." If any of you place religion in outward things, I shall not perhaps please you this morning; you will understand me no more when I speak of the work of God upon a poor sinner's heart, than if I were talking in an unknown tongue. I would further premise a caution, that I would by no means confine God to one way of acting. I would by no means say, that all persons, before they come to have a settled peace in their hearts, are obliged to undergo the same degrees of conviction. No; God has various ways of bringing his children home; his sacred Spirit bloweth when, and where, and how it listeth. But, however, I will venture to affirm this, that before ever you can speak peace to your heart, whether by shorter or longer continuance of your convictions, whether in a more pungent or in a more gentle way, you must undergo what I shall hereafter lay down in the following discourse.

First, then, before you can speak peace to your hearts, you must be made to see, made to feel, made to weep over, made to bewail, your actual transgressions against the law of God. According to the covenant of works, "The soul that sinneth it shall die; cursed is that man, be he what he may, that continueth not in all things that are written in the book of the law to do them." We are not only to do some things, but we are to do all things, and we are to continue so to do; so that the least deviation from the moral law, according to the covenant of works, whether in thought, word, or deed, deserves eternal death at the hand of God. And if one evil thought, if one evil word, if one evil action, deserves eternal damnation, how many hells, my friends, do every one of us deserve, whose whole lives have been one continued rebellion against God! Before ever, therefore, you can speak peace to your hearts, you must be brought to see, brought to believe, what a dreadful thing it is to depart from the living God. And now, my dear friends, examine your hearts, for I hope you came hither with a design to have your souls made better. Give me leave to ask you, in the presence of God, whether you know the time, and if you do not know exactly the time, do you know there was a time, when God wrote bitter things against you, when the arrows of the Almighty were within you? Was ever the remembrance of your sins grievous to you? Was the burden of your sins intolerable to your thoughts? Did you ever see that God's wrath might justly fall upon you, on account of your actual transgressions against God? Were you ever in all your life sorry for your sins? Could you ever say, My sins are gone over my head as a burden too heavy for me to bear? Did you ever experience any such thing as this? Did ever any such thing as this pass between God and your soul? If not, for Jesus Christ's sake, do not call yourselves Christians; you may speak peace to your hearts, but there is no peace. May the Lord awaken you, may the Lord convert you, may the Lord give you peace, if it be his will, before you go home!

But further: you may be convinced of your actual sins, so as to be made to tremble, and yet you may be strangers to Jesus Christ, you may have no true work of grace upon your hearts. Before ever, therefore, you can speak peace to your hearts, conviction must go deeper; you must not only be convinced of your actual transgressions against the law of God, but likewise of the foundation of all your transgressions. And what is that? I mean original sin, that original corruption each of us brings into the world with us, which renders us liable to God's wrath and damnation. There are many poor souls that think themselves fine reasoners, yet they pretend to say there is no such thing as original sin; they will charge God with injustice in imputing Adam's sin to us; although we have got the mark of the beast and of the devil upon us, yet they tell us we are not born in sin. Let them look abroad into the world and see the disorders in it, and think, if they can, if this is the paradise in which God did put man. No! everything in the world is out of order. I have often thought, when I was abroad, that if there were no other argument to prove original sin, the rising of wolves and tigers against man, nay, the barking of a dog against us, is a proof of original sin. Tigers and lions durst not rise against us, if it were not for Adam's first sin; for when the creatures rise up against us, it is as much as to say, You have sinned against God, and we take up our Master's quarrel. If we look inwardly, we shall see enough of lusts, and man's temper contrary to the temper of God. There is pride, malice, and revenge, in all our hearts; and this temper cannot come from God; it comes from our first parent, Adam, who, after he fell from God, fell out of God into the devil. However, therefore, some people may deny this, yet when conviction comes, all carnal reasonings are battered down immediately and the poor soul begins to feel and see the fountain from which all the polluted streams do flow. When the sinner is first awakened, he begins to wonder – How came I to be so wicked? The Spirit of God then strikes in, and shows that he has no good thing in him by nature; then he sees that he is altogether gone out of the way, that he is altogether become abominable, and the poor creature is made to live down at the foot of the throne of God, and to acknowledge that God would be just to damn him, just to cut him off, though he never had committed one actual sin in his life. Did you ever feel and experience this, any of you – to justify God in your damnation – to own that you are by nature children of wrath, and that God may justly cut you off, though you never actually had offended him in all your life? If you were ever truly convicted, if your hearts were ever truly cut, if self were truly taken out of you, you would be made to see and feel this. And if you have never felt the weight of original sin, do not call yourselves Christians. I am verily persuaded original sin is the greatest burden of a true convert; this ever grieves the regenerate soul, the sanctified soul. The indwelling of sin in the heart is the burden of a converted person; it is the burden of a true Christian. He continually cries out, "O! who will deliver me from this body of death," this indwelling corruption in my heart? This is that which disturbs a poor soul most. And, therefore, if you never felt this inward corruption, if you never saw that God might justly curse you for it, indeed, my dear friends, you may speak peace to your hearts, but I fear, nay, I know, there is no true peace.

Further: before you can speak peace to your hearts, you must not only be troubled for the sins of your life, the sin of your nature, but likewise for the sins of your best duties and performances. When a poor soul is somewhat awakened by the terrors of the Lord, then the poor creature, being born under the covenant of works, flies directly to a covenant of works again. And as Adam and Eve hid themselves among the trees of the garden, and sewed fig leaves together to cover their nakedness, so the poor sinner, when awakened, flies to his duties and to his performances, to hide himself from God, and goes to patch up a righteousness of his own. Says he, I will be mighty good now – I will reform – I will do all I can; and then certainly Jesus Christ will have mercy on me. But before you can speak peace to your heart, you must be brought to see that God may damn you for the best prayer you ever put up; you must be brought to see that all your duties – all your righteousness – as the prophet elegantly expresses it – put them all together, are so far from recommending you to God, are so far from being any motive and inducement to God to have mercy on your poor soul, that he will see them to be filthy rags, a menstruous cloth – that God hates them, and cannot away with them, if you bring them to him in order to recommend you to his favor. My dear friends, what is there in our performances to recommend us unto God? Our persons are in an unjustified state by nature, we deserve to be damned ten thousand times over; and what must our performances be? We can do no good thing by nature: "They that are in the flesh cannot please God." You may do many things materially good, but you cannot do a thing formally and rightly good; because nature cannot act above itself. It is impossible that a man who is unconverted can act for the glory of God; he cannot do anything in faith, and "whatsoever is not of faith is sin." After we are renewed, yet we are renewed but in part, indwelling sin continues in us, there is a mixture of corruption in every one of our duties; so that after we are converted, were Jesus Christ only to accept us according to our works, our works would damn us, for we cannot put up a prayer but it is far from that perfection which the moral law requireth. I do not know what you may think, but I can say that I cannot pray but I sin – I cannot preach to you or any others but I sin – I can do nothing without sin; and, as one expresseth it, my repentance wants to be repented of, and my tears to be washed in the precious blood of my dear Redeemer. Our best duties are as so many splendid sins. Before you can speak peace in your heart, you must not only be made sick of your original and actual sin, but you must be made sick of your righteousness, of all your duties and performances. There must be a deep conviction before you can be brought out of your self-righteousness; it is the last idol taken out of our heart. The pride of our heart will not let us submit to the righteousness of Jesus Christ. But if you never felt that you had no righteousness of your own, if you never felt the deficiency of your own righteousness, you cannot come to Jesus Christ. There are a great many now who may say, Well, we believe all this; but there is a great difference betwixt talking and feeling. Did you ever feel the want of a dear Redeemer? Did you ever feel the want of Jesus Christ, upon the account of the deficiency of your own righteousness? And can you now say from your heart, Lord, thou mayst justly damn me for the best duties that ever I did perform? If you are not thus brought out of self, you may speak peace to yourselves, but yet there is no peace.

But then, before you can speak peace to your souls, there is one particular sin you must be greatly troubled for, and yet I fear there are few of you think what it is; it is the reigning, the damning sin of the Christian world, and yet the Christian world seldom or never think of it. And pray what is that? It is what most of you think you are not guilty of – and that is, the sin of unbelief. Before you can speak peace to your heart, you must be troubled for the unbelief of your heart. But, can it be supposed that any of you are unbelievers here in this church-yard, that are born in Scotland, in a reformed country, that go to church every Sabbath? Can any of you that receive the sacrament once a year – O that it were administered oftener! – can it be supposed that you who had tokens for the sacrament, that you who keep up family prayer, that any of you do not believe in the Lord Jesus Christ? I appeal to your own hearts, if you would not think me uncharitable, if I doubted whether any of you believed in Christ; and yet, I fear upon examination, we should find that most of you have not so much faith in the Lord Jesus Christ as the devil himself. I am persuaded the devil believes more of the Bible than most of us do. He believes the divinity of Jesus Christ; that is more than many who call themselves Christians do; nay, he believes and trembles, and that is more than thousands amongst us do. My friends, we mistake a historical faith for a true faith, wrought in the heart by the Spirit of God. You fancy you believe, because you believe there is such a book as we call the Bible – because you go to church; all this you may do, and have no true faith in Christ. Merely to believe there was such a person as Christ, merely to believe there is a book called the Bible, will do you no good, more than to believe there was such a man as Caesar or Alexander the Great. The Bible is a sacred depository. What thanks have we to give to God for these lively oracles! But yet we may have these, and not believe in the Lord Jesus Christ. My dear friends, there must be a principle wrought in the heart by the Spirit of the living God. Did I ask you how long it is since you believed in Jesus

Christ, I suppose most of you would tell me, you believed in Jesus Christ as long as ever you remember — you never did misbelieve. Then, you could not give me a better proof that you never yet believed in Jesus Christ, unless you were sanctified early, as from the womb; for, they that otherwise believed in Christ know there was a time when they did not believe in Jesus Christ. You say you love God with all your heart, soul, and strength. If I were to ask you how long it is since you loved God, you would say, As long as you can remember; you never hated God, you know no time when there was enmity in your heart against God. Then, unless you were sanctified very early, you never loved God in your life. My dear friends, I am more particular in this, because it is a most deceitful delusion, whereby so many people are carried away, that they believe already. Therefore, it is remarked of Mr. Marshall, giving account of his experiences, that he had been working for life, and he had ranged all his sins under the ten commandments, and then coming to a minister, asked him the reason why he could not get peace. The minister looked at his catalogue, Away, says he, I do not find one word of the sin of unbelief in all your catalogue. It is the peculiar work of the Spirit of God to convince us of our unbelief – that we have got no faith. Says Jesus Christ, "I will send the Comforter; and when he is come, he will reprove the world" of the sin of unbelief; "of sin," says Christ, "because they believe not on me." Now, my dear friends, did God ever show you that you had no faith? Were you ever made to bewail a hard heart of unbelief? Was it ever the language of your heart, Lord, give me faith; Lord, enable me to lay hold on thee; Lord, enable me to call thee MY Lord and MY God? Did Jesus Christ ever convince you in this manner? Did he ever convince you of your inability to close with Christ, and make you to cry out to God to give you faith? If not, do not speak peace to your heart. May the Lord awaken you, and give you true, solid peace before you go hence and be no more!

Once more then: before you can speak peace to your heart, you must not only be convinced of your actual and original sin, the sins of your own righteousness, the sin of unbelief, but you must be enabled to lay hold upon the perfect righteousness, the all-sufficient righteousness, of the Lord Jesus Christ; you must lay hold by faith on the righteousness of Jesus Christ, and then you shall have peace. "Come," says Jesus, "unto me, all ye that are weary and heavy laden, and I will give you rest." This speaks encouragement to all that are weary and heavy laden; but the promise of rest is made to them only upon their coming and believing, and taking him to be their God and their all. Before we can ever have peace with God, we must be justified by faith through our Lord Jesus Christ, we must be enabled to apply Christ to our hearts, we must have Christ brought home to our souls, so as his righteousness may be made our righteousness, so as his merits may be imputed to our souls. My dear friends, were you ever married to Jesus Christ? Did Jesus Christ ever give himself to you? Did you ever close with Christ by a lively faith, so as to feel Christ in your hearts, so as to hear him speaking peace to your souls? Did peace ever flow in upon your hearts like a river? Did you ever feel that peace that Christ spoke to his disciples? I pray God he may come and speak peace to you. These things you must experience. I am not talking of the invisible realities of another world, of inward religion, of the work of God upon a poor sinner's heart. I am not talking of a matter of great importance, my dear hearers; you are all concerned in it, your souls are concerned in it, your eternal salvation is concerned in it. You may be all at peace, but perhaps the devil has lulled you asleep into a carnal lethargy and security, and will endeavor to keep you there, till he gets you to hell, and there you will be awakened; but it will be dreadful to be awakened and find yourselves so fearfully mistaken, when the great gulf is fixed, when you will be calling to all eternity for a drop of water to cool your tongue, and shall not obtain it.

Give me leave, then, to address myself to several sorts of persons; and O may God, of his infinite mercy, bless the application! There are some of you perhaps can say, Through grace we can go along with you. Blessed be God, we have been convinced of our actual sins, we have been convinced of original sin, we have been convinced of self-righteousness, we have felt the bitterness of unbelief, and through grace we have closed with Jesus Christ; we can speak peace to our hearts, because God hath spoken peace to us. Can you say so? Then I will salute you, as the angels did the women the first day of the week, All hail! Fear not ye, my dear brethren, you are happy souls; you may lie down and be at peace indeed, for God hath given you peace; you may be content under all the dispensations of providence, for nothing can happen to you now, but what shall be the effect of God's love to your soul; you need not fear what sightings may be without, seeing there is peace within. Have you closed with Christ? Is God your friend? Is Christ your friend? Then, look up with comfort; all is yours, and you are Christ's, and Christ is God's. Everything shall work together for your good; the very hairs of your head are numbered; he that toucheth you, toucheth the apple of God's eye. But then, my dear friends, beware of resting on your first conversion. You that are young believers in Christ, you should be looking out for fresh discoveries of the Lord Jesus Christ every moment; you must not build upon your past experiences, you must not build upon a work within you, but always come out of yourselves to the righteousness of Jesus Christ without you; you must be always coming as poor sinners to draw water out of the wells of salvation; you must be forgetting the things that are behind, and be continually pressing forward to the things that are before. My dear friends, you must keep up a tender, close walk with the Lord Jesus Christ.

There are many of us who lose our peace by our untender walk; something or other gets in betwixt Christ and us, and we fall into darkness; something or other steals our hearts from God, and this grieves the Holy Ghost, and the Holy Ghost leaves us to ourselves. Let me, therefore, exhort you that have got peace with God, to take care that you do not lose this peace. It is true, if you are once in Christ, you cannot finally fall from God: "There is no condemnation to them that are in Christ Jesus;" but if you cannot fall finally, you may fall foully, and may go with broken bones all your days. Take care of backslidings; for Jesus Christ's sake, do not grieve the Holy Ghost – you may never recover your comfort while you live. O take care of going a gadding and wandering from God, after you have closed with Jesus Christ. My dear friends, I have paid dear for backsliding. Our hearts are so cursedly wicked, that if you take not care, if you do not keep up a constant watch, your wicked hearts will deceive you, and draw you aside. It will be sad to be under the scourge of a correcting Father; witness the visitation of Job, David, and other saints in Scripture. Let me, therefore, exhort you that have got peace to keep a close walk with Christ.

I am grieved with the loose walk of those that are Christians, that have had discoveries of Jesus Christ; there is so little difference betwixt them and other people, that I scarce know which is the true Christian. Christians are afraid to speak of God – they run down with the stream; if they come into worldly company, they will talk of the world as if they were in their element; this you would not do when you had the first discoveries of Christ's love; you could talk then of Christ's love for ever, when the candle of the Lord shined upon your soul. That time has been when you had something to say for your dear Lord; but now you can go into company and hear others speaking about the world bold enough, and you are afraid of being laughed at if you speak for Jesus Christ. A great many people have grown conformists now in the worst sense of the word; they will cry out against the ceremonies of the church, as they may justly do; but then you are mighty fond of ceremonies in your behavior; you will conform to the world, which is a great deal worse. Many will stay till the devil brings up new fashions. Take care, then, not to be conformed to the world. What have Christians to do with the world? Christians should be singularly good, bold for their Lord, that all who are with you may take notice that you have been with Jesus. I would exhort you to come to a settlement in Jesus Christ, so as to have a continual abiding of God in your heart. We go a-building on our faith of adherence, and lost our comfort; but we should be growing up to a faith of assurance, to know that we are God's, and so walk in the comfort of the Holy Ghost and be edified. Jesus Christ is now much wounded in the house of his friends. Excuse me in being particular; for, my friends, it grieves me more that Jesus Christ should be wounded by his friends than by his enemies. We cannot expect anything else from Deists; but for such as have felt his power, to fall away, for them not to walk agreeably to the vocation where-with they are called — by these means we bring our Lord's religion into contempt, to be a byword among the heathen. For Christ's sake, if you know Christ keep close by him; if God has spoken peace, O keep that peace by looking up to Jesus Christ every moment. Such as have got peace with God, if you are under trials, fear not, all things shall work for your good; if you are under temptations, fear not, if he has spoken peace to your hearts, all these things shall be for your good.

But what shall I say to you that have got no peace with God? – and these are, perhaps, the most of this congregation: it makes me weep to think of it. Most of you, if you examine your hearts, must confess that God never yet spoke peace to you; you are children of the devil, if Christ is not in you, if God has not spoken peace to your heart. Poor soul! What a cursed condition are you in. I would not be in your case for ten thousand, thousand worlds. Why? You are just hanging over hell. What peace can you have when God is your enemy, when the wrath of God is abiding upon your poor soul? Awake, then, you that are sleeping in a false peace, awake, ye carnal professors, ye hypocrites that go to church, receive the sacrament, read your Bibles, and never felt the power of God upon your hearts; you that are formal professors, you that are baptized heathens; awake, awake, and do not rest on a false bottom. Blame me not for addressing myself to you; indeed, it is out of love to your souls. I see you are lingering in your Sodom, and wanting to stay there; but I come to you as the angel did to Lot, to take you by the hand. Come away, my dear brethren – fly, fly, fly for your lives to Jesus Christ, fly to a bleeding God, fly to a throne of grace; and beg of God to break your hearts, beg of God to convince you of your actual sins, beg of God to convince you of your original sin, beg of God to convince you of your self-righteousness – beg of God to give you faith, and to enable you to close with Jesus Christ.

O you that are secure, I must be a son of thunder to you, and O that God may awaken you, though it be with thunder; it is out of love, indeed, that I speak to you. I know by sad experience what it is to be lulled asleep with a false peace; long was I lulled asleep, long did I think myself a Christian, when I knew nothing of the Lord Jesus Christ. I went perhaps farther than many of you do; I used to fast twice a-week, I used to pray sometimes nine times a-day, I used to receive the sacrament constantly every Lord's-day; and yet I knew nothing of Jesus Christ in my heart, I knew not that I must be a new creature – I knew nothing of inward religion in my soul. And perhaps, many of you may be deceived as I, poor creature, was; and, therefore, it is out of love to you indeed, that I speak to you. O if you do not take care, a form of religion will destroy your soul; you will rest in it, and will not come to Jesus Christ at all; whereas, these things are only the means, and not the end of religion; Christ is the end of the law for righteousness to all that believe. O, then, awake, you that are settled on your lees; awake you Church professors; awake you that have got a name to live, that are rich and think you want nothing, not considering that you are poor, and blind, and naked; I counsel you to come and buy of Jesus Christ gold, white raiment, and eye-salve. But I hope there are some that are a little wounded; I hope God does not intend to let me preach in vain; I hope God will reach some of your precious souls, and awaken some of you out of your carnal security; I hope there are some who are willing to come to Christ, and beginning to think that they have been building upon a false foundation. Perhaps the devil may strike in, and bid you despair of mercy; but fear not, what I have been speaking to you is only out of love to you – is only to awaken you, and let you see your danger.

If any of you are willing to be reconciled to God, God the Father, Son, and Holy Ghost, is willing to be reconciled to you. O then, though you have no peace as yet, come away to Jesus Christ; he is our peace, he is our peace-maker – he has made peace betwixt God and offending man. Would you have peace with God? Away, then, to God through Jesus Christ, who has purchased peace; the Lord Jesus has shed his heart's blood for this. He died for this; he rose again for this; he ascended into the highest heaven, and is now interceding at the right hand of God. Perhaps you think there will be no peace for you. Why so? Because you are sinners? Because you have crucified Christ – you have put him to open shame – you have trampled under foot the blood of the Son of God? What of all this? Yet there is peace for you. Pray, what did Jesus Christ say of his disciples, when he came to them the first day of the week? The first word he said was, "Peace be unto you;" he showed them his hands and his side, and said, "Peace be unto you." It is as much as if he had said, Fear not, my disciples; see my hands and my feet how they have been pierced for your sake; therefore fear not. How did Christ speak to his disciples? "Go tell my brethren, and tell broken-hearted Peter in particular, that Christ is risen, that he is ascended unto his Father and your Father, to his God and your God." And after Christ rose from the dead, he came preaching peace, with an olive branch of peace, like Noah's dove; "My peace I leave with you." Who were they? They were enemies of Christ as well as we, they were deniers of Christ once as well as we. Perhaps some of you have backslidden and lost your peace, and you think you deserve no peace; and no more you do. But, then, God will heal your backslidings, he will love you freely. As for you that are wounded, if you are made willing to come to Christ, come away.

Perhaps some of you want to dress yourselves in your duties, that are but rotten rags. No, you had better come naked as you are, for you must throw aside your rags, and come in your blood. Some of you may say, We would come, but we have got a hard heart. But you will never get it made soft till ye come to Christ; he will take away the heart of stone, and give you a heart of flesh; he will speak peace to your souls; though ye have betrayed him, yet he will be your peace. Shall I prevail upon any of you this morning to come to Jesus Christ? There is a great multitude of souls here; how shortly must you all die, and go to judgment! Even before night, or to-morrow's night, some of you may be laid out for this kirk-yard. And how will you do if you be not at peace with God – if the Lord Jesus Christ has not spoken peace to your heart? If God speak not peace to you here, you will be damned for ever. I must not flatter you, my dear friends; I will deal sincerely with your souls. Some of you may think I carry things too far. But, indeed, when you come to judgment, you will find what I say is true, either to your eternal damnation or comfort. May God influence your hearts to come to him! I am not willing to go away without persuading you. I cannot be persuaded but God may make use of me as a means of persuading some of you to come to the Lord Jesus Christ. O did you but feel the peace which they have that love the Lord Jesus Christ! "Great peace have they," say the psalmist, "that love thy law; nothing shall offend them." But there is no peace to the wicked.

I know what it is to live a life of sin; I was obliged to sin in order to stifle conviction. And I am sure this is the way many of you take; If you get into company, you drive off conviction. But you had better go to the bottom at once; it must be done – your wound must be searched, or you must be damned. If it were a matter of indifference, I would not speak one word about it. But you will be damned without Christ. He is the way, he is the truth, and the life. I cannot think you should go to hell without Christ. How can you dwell with everlasting burnings? How can you abide the thought of living with the devil for ever? Is it not better to have some soul-trouble here, than to be sent to hell by Jesus Christ hereafter? What is hell, but to be absent from Christ? If there were no other hell, that would be hell enough. It will be hell to be tormented with the devil for ever. Get acquaintance with God, then, and be at peace. I beseech you, as a poor worthless ambassador of Jesus Christ, that you would be reconciled to God. My business this morning, the first day of the week, is to tell you that Christ is willing to be reconciled to you. Will any of you be reconciled to Jesus Christ? Then, he will forgive you all your sins, he will blot out all your transgressions. But if you will go on and rebel against Christ, and stab him daily – if you will go on and abuse Jesus Christ, the wrath of God you must expect will fall upon you. God will not be mocked; that which a man soweth, that shall he also reap. And if you will not be at peace with God, God will not be at peace with you. Who can stand before God when he is angry? It is a dreadful thing to fall into the hands of an angry God. When the people came to apprehend Christ, they fell to the ground when Jesus said, "I am he." And if they could not bear the sight of Christ when clothed with the rags of mortality, how will they bear the sight of him when he is on his Father's throne?

Methinks I see the poor wretches dragged out of their graves by the devil; methinks I see them trembling, crying out to the hills and rocks to cover them. But the devil will say, Come, I will take you away; and then they shall stand trembling before the judgment-seat of Christ. They shall appear before him to see him once, and hear him pronounce that irrevocable sentence, "Depart from me, ye cursed." Methinks I hear the poor creatures saying, Lord, if we must be damned, let some angel pronounce the sentence. No, the God of love, Jesus Christ, will pronounce it. Will ye not believe this? Do not think I am talking at random, but agreeably to the Scriptures of truth. If you do not, then show yourselves men, and this morning go away with full resolution, in the strength of God, to cleave to Christ. And may you have no rest in your souls till you rest in Jesus Christ! I could still go on, for it is sweet to talk of Christ. Do you not long for the time when you shall have new bodies – when they shall be immortal, and made like Christ's glorious body? And then they will talk of Jesus Christ for evermore. But it is time, perhaps, for you to go and prepare for your respective worship, and I would not hinder any of you. My design is, to bring poor sinners to Jesus Christ. O that God may bring some of you to himself! May the Lord Jesus now dismiss you with his blessing, and may the dear Redeemer convince you that are unawakened, and turn the wicked from the evil of their way! And may the love of God, that passeth all under-standing, fill your hearts. Grant this, O Father, for Christ's sake; to whom, with thee and the blessed Spirit, be all honor and glory, now and for evermore. Amen.

Review Questions
1. What, according to Whitefield, is the greatest curse upon a people?
2. With what does God charge false ministers?
3. What did Whitefield mean when he accused ministers of "stifling people's convictions"?
4. How did Whitefield categorize religion?
5. Did Whitefield think everyone should have the same degree of conviction?
6. Why did Whitefield warn against false peace?
7. What are the steps to God's inward peace?

Thought Questions
1. How can you tell the difference between God's and the devil's peace?
2. Do you agree with Whitefield's steps to reaching salvation? Defend your answer.
3. Whitefield said, "Beware of resting on your first conversion...you must not build upon a work within you." What does he mean? Do you agree?
4. What is the difference between falling finally and falling foully away from God?
5. Have you ever begged God to break your heart? What does that mean to you? What does it look like when God breaks someone's heart?

Reading Skills
THEMES

Whitefield's sermon is lengthy, but it is largely focused on a few key themes. Notice that the sermon begins by quoting the Biblical passage it will address. Using that general theme as a starting point, try to identify other major themes of the sermon.

Watch for places in which Whitefield guides his argument back to his main points. What techniques does he use to reiterate and reinforce his theme? Pay particular attention to the first and last sentences of each paragraph.

Based on the information you have gathered, try to summarize the main point of the sermon in three sentences or less. Ask yourself if Whitefield effectively conveys his message or if his sermon strays too far from its main argument. Think about how you as a writer can stay focused on your argument.

"Paul Revere's Ride"

Henry W. Longfellow

Henry Wadsworth Longfellow (1807-1882) grew up in Maine during the War of 1812. He published his first poem when he was only thirteen years old. As an aspiring poet, he traveled and read widely before he settled in Massachusetts and became a prolific (and famous) writer of both poetry and novels. "Paul Revere's Ride" was written in 1860 and published in 1863 in the collection *Tales of a Wayside Inn*. The poem, which is largely historical, described the events of April 18, 1775, and it raised the name of the silversmith Paul Revere (c. 1734-1818) out of relative obscurity to that of a national hero.

Listen my children and you shall hear
Of the midnight ride of Paul Revere,
On the eighteenth of April, in Seventy-five;
Hardly a man is now alive
Who remembers that famous day and year.

He said to his friend, "If the British march
By land or sea from the town to-night,
Hang a lantern aloft in the belfry arch
Of the North Church tower as a signal light, —
One if by land, and two if by sea;
And I on the opposite shore will be,
Ready to ride and spread the alarm
Through every Middlesex village and farm,
For the country folk to be up and to arm."

Then he said "Good-night!" and with muffled oar
Silently rowed to the Charlestown shore,
Just as the moon rose over the bay,
Where swinging wide at her moorings lay

The *Somerset*, British man-of-war;
A phantom ship, with each mast and spar
Across the moon like a prison bar,
And a huge black hulk, that was magnified
By its own reflection in the tide.

Meanwhile, his friend through alley and street
Wanders and watches, with eager ears,
Till in the silence around him he hears
The muster of men at the barrack door,
The sound of arms, and the tramp of feet,
And the measured tread of the grenadiers,
Marching down to their boats on the shore.

Then he climbed the tower of the Old North Church,
By the wooden stairs, with stealthy tread,
To the belfry chamber overhead,
And startled the pigeons from their perch
On the sombre rafters, that round him made
Masses and moving shapes of shade, —
By the trembling ladder, steep and tall,
To the highest window in the wall,
Where he paused to listen and look down
A moment on the roofs of the town
And the moonlight flowing over all.

Beneath, in the churchyard, lay the dead,
In their night encampment on the hill,
Wrapped in silence so deep and still
That he could hear, like a sentinel's tread,
The watchful night-wind, as it went
Creeping along from tent to tent,
And seeming to whisper, "All is well!"
A moment only he feels the spell
Of the place and the hour, and the secret dread
Of the lonely belfry and the dead;
For suddenly all his thoughts are bent
On a shadowy something far away,
Where the river widens to meet the bay, —
A line of black that bends and floats
On the rising tide like a bridge of boats.

Meanwhile, impatient to mount and ride,
Booted and spurred, with a heavy stride

On the opposite shore walked Paul Revere.
Now he patted his horse's side,
Now he gazed at the landscape far and near,
Then, impetuous, stamped the earth,
And turned and tightened his saddle girth;
But mostly he watched with eager search
The belfry tower of the Old North Church,
As it rose above the graves on the hill,
Lonely and spectral and sombre and still.
And lo! as he looks, on the belfry's height
A glimmer, and then a gleam of light!
He springs to the saddle, the bridle he turns,
But lingers and gazes, till full on his sight
A second lamp in the belfry burns.

A hurry of hoofs in a village street,
A shape in the moonlight, a bulk in the dark,
And beneath, from the pebbles, in passing, a spark
Struck out by a steed flying fearless and fleet;
That was all! And yet, through the gloom and the light,
The fate of a nation was riding that night;
And the spark struck out by that steed, in his flight,
Kindled the land into flame with its heat.

He has left the village and mounted the
steep,
And beneath him, tranquil and broad and
deep,
Is the Mystic, meeting the ocean tides;
And under the alders that skirt its edge,
Now soft on the sand, now loud on the
ledge,
Is heard the tramp of his steed as he rides.

It was twelve by the village clock
When he crossed the bridge into Medford
town.
He heard the crowing of the cock,
And the barking of the farmer's dog,
And felt the damp of the river fog,
That rises after the sun goes down.

It was one by the village clock,
When he galloped into Lexington.

He saw the gilded weathercock
Swim in the moonlight as he passed,
And the meeting-house windows, black and bare,
Gaze at him with a spectral glare,
As if they already stood aghast
At the bloody work they would look upon.

It was two by the village clock,
When he came to the bridge in Concord town.
He heard the bleating of the flock,
And the twitter of birds among the trees,
And felt the breath of the morning breeze
Blowing over the meadow brown.
And one was safe and asleep in his bed
Who at the bridge would be first to fall,
Who that day would be lying dead,
Pierced by a British musket ball.

You know the rest. In the books you have read
How the British Regulars fired and fled, —
How the farmers gave them ball for ball,
From behind each fence and farmyard wall,
Chasing the redcoats down the lane,
Then crossing the fields to emerge again
Under the trees at the turn of the road,
And only pausing to fire and load.

So through the night rode Paul Revere;
And so through the night went his cry of alarm
To every Middlesex village and farm, —
A cry of defiance, and not of fear,
A voice in the darkness, a knock at the door,
And a word that shall echo for evermore!
For, borne on the night-wind of the Past,
Through all our history, to the last,
In the hour of darkness and peril and need,
The people will waken and listen to hear
The hurrying hoof-beats of that steed,
And the midnight message of Paul Revere.

Review Questions

1. What did the signals from the North Church mean?
2. Which way did the British come?
3. What was the outcome of that day's battle?
4. Describe the structure of this poem. Does Longfellow use rhyme? If so, does every line rhyme? Which ones do?
5. What kind of images does the poem use? To which of the five senses does it appeal?

Thought Questions

1. Why do you think Longfellow focused on Paul Revere out of all the events of that night?
2. Was the "fate of a nation" riding that night? What if Paul Revere had not ridden?
3. Why does it take someone like Paul Revere to stir a people into flame?
4. Paul Revere gained national prominence through Longfellow's poem. Does that information make Revere less of a hero? Why or why not?

Reading Skills
TIMELINE

"Paul Revere's Ride" gives you the chance to draw out a very specific timeline, focusing on hours of the night rather than days or weeks. For each point on your timeline, jot down what Paul Revere was doing at that time. If the poem does not directly say, give an estimate.

As you write your timeline, think about the way Longfellow uses time in his poem. Does he seem to stretch it out or make it pass quickly? What effect does this have on the mood of the poem? If you were going to write an essay about "Paul Revere's Ride," think about the kind of arguments you could make regarding the poem's use of time.

"The Song of Hiawatha" (excerpt)
Henry W. Longfellow

"The Song of Hiawatha" is another famous poem by Longfellow. This piece demonstrates the poet's interest in the local history of America: Longfellow collected legends about the Ojibway Native American tribes and wrote this lengthy poem based on his findings. The poem was first published in 1855, and it was divided into twenty-two parts plus an introduction. This selection from the introduction and part one gives you a general idea of the tone of the poem.

Introduction

Should you ask me,
Whence these stories?
Whence these legends and traditions,
With the odors of the forest
With the dew and damp of meadows,
With the curling smoke of wigwams,
With the rushing of great rivers,
With their frequent repetitions,
And their wild reverberations
As of thunder in the mountains?

I should answer, I should tell you,
"From the forests and the prairies,
From the great lakes of the Northland,
From the land of the Ojibways,
From the land of the Dacotahs,
From the mountains, moors, and fen-lands
Where the heron, the Shuh-shuh-gah,
Feeds among the reeds and rushes.
I repeat them as I heard them

From the lips of Nawadaha,
The musician, the sweet singer."

Should you ask where Nawadaha
Found these songs so wild and wayward,
Found these legends and traditions,
I should answer, I should tell you,
"In the bird's-nests of the forest,
In the lodges of the beaver,
In the hoofprint of the bison,
In the eyry of the eagle!

"All the wild-fowl sang them to him,
In the moorlands and the fen-lands,
In the melancholy marshes;
Chetowaik, the plover, sang them,
Mahng, the loon, the wild-goose, Wawa,
The blue heron, the Shuh-shuh-gah,
And the grouse, the Mushkodasa!"

If still further you should ask me,
Saying, "Who was Nawadaha?
Tell us of this Nawadaha,"
I should answer your inquiries
Straightway in such words as follow.

"In the vale of Tawasentha,
In the green and silent valley,
By the pleasant water-courses,
Dwelt the singer Nawadaha.
Round about the Indian village
Spread the meadows and the corn-fields,
And beyond them stood the forest,
Stood the groves of singing pine-trees,
Green in Summer, white in Winter,
Ever sighing, ever singing.

"And the pleasant water-courses,
You could trace them through the valley,
By the rushing in the Spring-time,
By the alders in the Summer,
By the white fog in the Autumn,
By the black line in the Winter;
And beside them dwelt the singer,
In the vale of Tawasentha,
In the green and silent valley.

"There he sang of Hiawatha,
Sang the Song of Hiawatha,
Sang his wondrous birth and being,
How he prayed and how be fasted,
How he lived, and toiled, and suffered,
That the tribes of men might prosper,
That he might advance his people!"

Ye who love the haunts of Nature,
Love the sunshine of the meadow,
Love the shadow of the forest,
Love the wind among the branches,
And the rain-shower and the snow-storm,
And the rushing of great rivers
Through their palisades of pine-trees,
And the thunder in the mountains,
Whose innumerable echoes
Flap like eagles in their eyries;-
Listen to these wild traditions,
To this Song of Hiawatha!

Ye who love a nation's legends,
Love the ballads of a people,
That like voices from afar off
Call to us to pause and listen,
Speak in tones so plain and childlike,
Scarcely can the ear distinguish
Whether they are sung or spoken;-
Listen to this Indian Legend,
To this Song of Hiawatha!
Ye whose hearts are fresh and simple,
Who have faith in God and Nature,
Who believe that in all ages
Every human heart is human,
That in even savage bosoms
There are longings, yearnings, strivings
For the good they comprehend not,

That the feeble hands and helpless,
Groping blindly in the darkness,
Touch God's right hand in that darkness
And are lifted up and strengthened;-
Listen to this simple story,
To this Song of Hiawatha!

Ye, who sometimes, in your rambles
Through the green lanes of the country,
Where the tangled barberry-bushes
Hang their tufts of crimson berries
Over stone walls gray with mosses,
Pause by some neglected graveyard,
For a while to muse, and ponder
On a half-effaced inscription,
Written with little skill of song-craft,
Homely phrases, but each letter
Full of hope and yet of heart-break,
Full of all the tender pathos
Of the Here and the Hereafter;
Stay and read this rude inscription,
Read this Song of Hiawatha!

Part I

The Peace-Pipe

On the Mountains of the Prairie,
On the great Red Pipe-stone Quarry,
Gitche Manito, the mighty,
He the Master of Life, descending,
On the red crags of the quarry
Stood erect, and called the nations,
Called the tribes of men together.

From his footprints flowed a river,
Leaped into the light of morning,
O'er the precipice plunging downward
Gleamed like Ishkoodah, the comet.
And the Spirit, stooping earthward,
With his finger on the meadow
Traced a winding pathway for it,
Saying to it, "Run in this way!"

From the red stone of the quarry
With his hand he broke a fragment,
Moulded it into a pipe-head,
Shaped and fashioned it with figures;
From the margin of the river
Took a long reed for a pipe-stem,
With its dark green leaves upon it;
Filled the pipe with bark of willow,
With the bark of the red willow;

Breathed upon the neighboring forest,
Made its great boughs chafe together,
Till in flame they burst and kindled;
And erect upon the mountains,
Gitche Manito, the mighty,
Smoked the calumet, the Peace-Pipe,
As a signal to the nations.

And the smoke rose slowly, slowly,
Through the tranquil air of morning,
First a single line of darkness,
Then a denser, bluer vapor,
Then a snow-white cloud unfolding,
Like the tree-tops of the forest,
Ever rising, rising, rising,
Till it touched the top of heaven,
Till it broke against the heaven,
And rolled outward all around it.

From the Vale of Tawasentha,
From the Valley of Wyoming,
From the groves of Tuscaloosa,
From the far-off Rocky Mountains,
From the Northern lakes and rivers
All the tribes beheld the signal,
Saw the distant smoke ascending,
The Pukwana of the Peace-Pipe.

And the Prophets of the nations
Said: "Behold it, the Pukwana!
By the signal of the Peace-Pipe,
Bending like a wand of willow,
Waving like a hand that beckons,
Gitche Manito, the mighty,
Calls the tribes of men together,
Calls the warriors to his council!"

Down the rivers, o'er the prairies,
Came the warriors of the nations,
Came the Delawares and Mohawks,
Came the Choctaws and Camanches,
Came the Shoshonies and Blackfeet,
Came the Pawnees and Omahas,
Came the Mandans and Dacotahs,
Came the Hurons and Ojibways,
All the warriors drawn together

By the signal of the Peace-Pipe,
To the Mountains of the Prairie,
To the great Red Pipe-stone Quarry,

And they stood there on the meadow,
With their weapons and their war-gear,
Painted like the leaves of Autumn,
Painted like the sky of morning,
Wildly glaring at each other;
In their faces stem defiance,
In their hearts the feuds of ages,
The hereditary hatred,
The ancestral thirst of vengeance.

Gitche Manito, the mighty,
The creator of the nations,
Looked upon them with compassion,
With paternal love and pity;
Looked upon their wrath and wrangling
But as quarrels among children,
But as feuds and fights of children!

Over them he stretched his right hand,
To subdue their stubborn natures,
To allay their thirst and fever,
By the shadow of his right hand;
Spake to them with voice majestic

As the sound of far-off waters,
Falling into deep abysses,
Warning, chiding, spake in this wise:

"O my children! my poor children!
Listen to the words of wisdom,
Listen to the words of warning,
From the lips of the Great Spirit,
From the Master of Life, who made you!

"I have given you lands to hunt in,
I have given you streams to fish in,
I have given you bear and bison,
I have given you roe and reindeer,
I have given you brant and beaver,
Filled the marshes full of wild-fowl,
Filled the rivers full of fishes:
Why then are you not contented?
Why then will you hunt each other?

"I am weary of your quarrels,
Weary of your wars and bloodshed,
Weary of your prayers for vengeance,
Of your wranglings and dissensions;
All your strength is in your union,
All your danger is in discord;
Therefore be at peace henceforward,
And as brothers live together.

"I will send a Prophet to you,
A Deliverer of the nations,
Who shall guide you and shall teach you,
Who shall toil and suffer with you.
If you listen to his counsels,
You will multiply and prosper;
If his warnings pass unheeded,
You will fade away and perish!

"Bathe now in the stream before you,
Wash the war-paint from your faces,
Wash the blood-stains from your fingers,
Bury your war-clubs and your weapons,
Break the red stone from this quarry,
Mould and make it into Peace-Pipes,
Take the reeds that grow beside you,
Deck them with your brightest feathers,
Smoke the calumet together,
And as brothers live henceforward!"

Then upon the ground the warriors
Threw their cloaks and shirts of deer-skin,
Threw their weapons and their war-gear,
Leaped into the rushing river,
Washed the war-paint from their faces.
Clear above them flowed the water,
Clear and limpid from the footprints
Of the Master of Life descending;
Dark below them flowed the water,
Soiled and stained with streaks of crimson,
As if blood were mingled with it!

From the river came the warriors,
Clean and washed from all their war-paint;
On the banks their clubs they buried,

Buried all their warlike weapons.
Gitche Manito, the mighty,
The Great Spirit, the creator,
Smiled upon his helpless children!
And in silence all the warriors
Broke the red stone of the quarry,
Smoothed and formed it into Peace-Pipes,
Broke the long reeds by the river,

Decked them with their brightest feathers,
And departed each one homeward,
While the Master of Life, ascending,

Through the opening of cloud-curtains,
 Through the doorways of the heaven,

Vanished from before their faces,
In the smoke that rolled around him,
The Pukwana of the Peace-Pipe!

Review Questions

1. Where did the legends come from?
2. Who was Nawadaha?
3. Who was the Master of Life?
4. What did the smoke of the peace pipe signify?
5. What did Gitche Manito warn the tribes? What did he ask them to do?

Thought Questions

1. How do legends begin? How are they passed on?
2. What are some legends today? Do they have the same power they used to? Why or why not?
3. What does it mean to have faith in Nature?
4. Why do people fight each other? Be prepared to defend your answer.
5. How is what Gitche Manito said different from what God might say to the world? How is it similar?

Reading Skills
CHARACTERS

When you begin to write about literature, you will find it helpful if you can master the ability to learn characters' names and relationships to each other. You don't want to write an entire paper and then discover that your thesis is invalid because you mixed up two of the main characters. This kind of memory work does not come automatically, however; the best way to acquire that skill is to practice with works of literature—like this one—that have a lot of characters, especially if they have similar-sounding names.

In this poem, the unfamiliar names of the characters may be confusing, so as you read, take a minute to write down each name that appears and give a brief, one- or two-sentence description of that character, based on the poem. Also note if the poem mentions the relationships between the characters. Later, you will be able to look back at your list and remember who it was that spoke that last, memorable speech, and how he or she was presented at the beginning of the poem.

The Sign of the Beaver
Elizabeth G. Speare

Elizabeth George Speare (1908-1994) began writing as a child growing up in New England, and as an adult, she drew most of her writing material out of the region's history. Although she started her career writing magazine articles, Speare eventually found her niche writing children's historical fiction. Although she wrote a relatively small number of books, she is one of the few American authors to have won more than one Newbery Medal for children's literature. Speare won in 1959 with *The Witch of Blackbird Pond*, and then won again in 1962 with her novel *The Bronze Bow*. *The Sign of the Beaver*, set in the wilderness outside colonial New England, was published in 1984, and received a Newbery Honor citation that same year.

Chapter 1

Review Questions
1. Why was Matt left alone?
2. What had Matt's father advised him to do? What had he given Matt?

Thought Questions
1. How long is the longest you have been left alone? Did time pass slowly or quickly?
2. Are you more likely to lose track of time if it moves fast or slowly?

Chapter 2

Review Questions
1. What were the annoyances in Matt's life?
2. How had Matt's father advised him to treat Indians?
3. What did Matt unexpectedly miss the most?

Thought Questions
1. Are you more likely to respect those you fear or those you love?

Chapter 3

Review Questions
1. Who arrived at the cabin?
2. Why did Matt lie to him?
3. Where was the stranger heading?
4. What did the stranger take with him when he left?

Thought Questions
1. In Matt's situation, how would you decide who to trust?

Chapter 4

Review Questions
1. What did Matt find when he came back from fishing?
2. Who/what had caused the damage?

Chapter 5

Review Questions
1. What did Matt determine to get? What happened when he tried?
2. Who rescued him?

Chapter 6

Review Questions
1. Whom did the Indian bring with him the second day?
2. What did the Indian give Matt?
3. What treaty did Saknis propose?

Thought Questions
1. Why didn't Matt think of lying to the Indian?
2. Why was Attean opposed to learning to read?

Chapter 7

Review Questions
1. How did Matt attempt to teach Attean? Why was Attean confused?
2. Why did Attean leave?

Chapter 8

Review Questions
1. What new tactic did Matt try in his teaching?
2. Why did Attean disapprove of the book?

Chapter 9

Review Questions
1. How had Attean killed the rabbit?
2. What kept Attean from learning faster?
3. Why did Attean become angry at the book?

2. Can you think of an exception?

Chapter 20

Review Questions
1. Why had Attean stayed away so long? Where was he going?
2. What did it mean if Attean could not find what he sought?

Thought Questions
1. Does your culture have any similar "rite of passage" into adulthood like Attean's?

Chapter 21

Review Questions
1. How was Attean different when he returned? Why was he leaving?
2. What did Saknis ask Matt to do?
3. What was Matt's response?

Thought Questions
1. What would you have chosen, if given the same choice Matt faced? Why?
2. Does your answer depend on whether you are a girl or a boy? Explain.
3. Are you bound to your family? If so, how?

Chapter 22

Review Questions
1. What gift had Saknis sent for Matt? What had Attean's grandmother sent?
2. Before he left, what did Attean give Matt?
3. What did Matt give Attean?

Thought Questions
1. Why did Attean say his people would not return in the spring?
2. Attean asked, "How can man own land? Land same as air. Land for all people to live on. For beaver and deer. Does deer own land?" Do you agree with Attean? Discuss.

Chapter 23

Review Questions
1. How did Matt pass the time after Attean left?
2. How did Matt get the fur for a fur hat?
3. What gifts did Matt make for his family?

Thought Questions
1. Why couldn't girls go to school in Matt's time? Did white girls receive any more respect than Indian girls?

Chapter 24

Thought Questions
1. Why did mastering the snowshoes make Matt unafraid of winter? What did they symbolize?

Chapter 25

Review Questions
1. When did Matt's family arrive? What had delayed them?
2. Where was the baby?
3. Why wasn't Matt pleased at the coming of neighbors?

Thought Questions
1. Why did Matt think his family would never understand about the Indians?
2. Does this book have a happy ending? Why or why not?

Brain Work
ASKING A QUESTION

Imagine you were going to write a paper about *The Sign of the Beaver*. Keeping in mind what you have learned about asking a good essay question, come up with a question that you might use to start an essay in each of the following categories.*

Example: Plot – Would Matt have survived on his own if he had not met Saknis and Attean?

1. Characters –

2. Themes –

3. Philosophy (of the characters or the author) –

4. Historical events –

5. Cultural attitudes –

Hint – use the Thought Questions about this book to jump-start your ideas.

The Witch of Blackbird Pond

Elizabeth G. Speare

Elizabeth George Speare (1908-1994) was born in Massachusetts, where, as a high school student, she began to compose short stories. Speare went on to become a high school English teacher before returning to writing. After her own children were in school, Speare began to write magazine articles about parenting and other topics. Her interest in New England's history eventually led her to write historical fiction for children, and she published her first novel, *Calico Captive*, in 1957. Speare won the first of two Newbery Medals in 1959 for *The Witch of Blackbird Pond*, which had been published in 1958, and which gives an account of the Salem witch trials.

Chapter 1

Review Questions
1. When and where does the book begin?
2. Who was Nathaniel Eaton?
3. Why was Kit disappointed by America?
4. What happened on the longboat on the way back to the *Dolphin* at Saybrook? Why was Kit reprimanded for her actions?
5. Why was John Holbrook going to Wethersfield?

Thought Questions
1. What do you associate with colonial America? Does Speare's portrayal surprise you?
2. What was the water trial? What is the logical problem with such a test?

Chapter 2

Review Questions
1. Describe the Cruff family.
2. What had prevented John Holbrook from attending Harvard?
3. Why had Kit come to New England?

    4. Why were Kit's aunt and uncle not waiting for her at Wethersfield?

Thought Questions
    1. What do John's views on work and study tell you about his desires? His expectations?
    2. Nat was scornful about the process of transporting slaves, but Kit was not. Why? Is "custom" an excuse for accepting unethical actions?
    3. John said the proper use of reading was "to improve our sinful nature and to fill our minds with God's holy word." Do you agree?

Chapter 3

Review Questions
    1. How was Kit received by the Woods?
    2. Why had Kit been forced to leave Barbados?
    3. What made Kit's two cousins so different?

Thought Questions
    1. Were the colonial Americans, as Kit asked, also subjects of King James?
    2. Why might Uncle Matthew have found that question offensive?

Chapter 4

Review Questions
    1. Why was Uncle Matthew offended by Kit's gifts?
    2. What was Uncle Matthew's one "weakness"?
    3. Why did Kit struggle to complete household tasks?

Thought Questions
    1. Why did Judith resent the time Rachel spent helping others in the community? What does her reaction tell you about her character?
    2. What does Uncle Matthew's reaction to the gifts suggest about his beliefs?

Chapter 5

Review Questions
    1. How did Kit anger Uncle Matthew on Sunday morning?
    2. Describe the town. Why did Kit find it surprising?
    3. What did it mean for a girl to "set her cap" for someone?

Thought Questions
    1. What do the town's Sabbath traditions tell you about the Puritans' values?
    2. At this point in the novel, are you led to sympathize with Kit or with Uncle Matthew? How do you know? What point does the novel seem to be making about Puritan culture?

Chapter 6

Review Questions
    1. Why did Uncle Matthew disapprove of Dr. Bulkeley?
    2. How had John Holbrook changed since he had been at Wethersfield?
    3. What request had William Ashby made of Uncle Matthew?
    4. Why wasn't Judith upset by Uncle Matthew's news?

Thought Questions
1. What does *allegiance* mean? How do people develop their allegiances?
2. Do you agree with Uncle Matthew that some things are worse than revolution? Is it possible to fight for your rights without bloodshed?
3. When are (human) (civil) (political) rights more important than non-violence? Discuss.
4. Was it reasonable for Dr. Bulkeley to consider Mercy weak? Why did Kit disagree?

Chapter 7

Review Questions
1. What did William seem to expect when he came calling?
2. Why had the assembly voted to leave no unclaimed land in Hartford?
3. Why was the charter so important?
4. Why was Judith sure William would return?

Thought Questions
1. How would you describe William and Kit's courtship? How are the expectations for male-female relationships different today?
2. What is *justice*? What does it take to truly understand it?
3. What does this novel imply about the Puritans' views of work and leisure? How do your own ideas differ?

Chapter 8

Review Questions
1. Why did no one live in the Great Meadow?
2. Who lived in the little house by Blackbird Pond?
3. What had Dr. Bulkeley recommended to the selectmen that Kit should do?
4. What was a Dame School?
5. What had happened to Uncle Matthew and Aunt Rachel's sons?

Chapter 9

Review Questions
1. What resources did Mercy and Kit use to teach?
2. How did Kit teach the story of the Good Samaritan?
3. Who interrupted her lesson? What did he threaten, and why?
4. Where did Kit go when she fled? Whom did she meet there?

Thought Questions
1. Where are teaching methods learned today? What are some of the main differences?
2. Why might acting be seen as scandalous to the Puritans?
3. Why were Hannah and others like her persecuted?

Chapter 10

Review Questions
1. How did Kit convince Mr. Kimberley to let the school remain open?
2. Why was Hannah Tupper considered an outcast?

3. What kind of fines was Hannah required to pay?
4. Who surprised Kit at Hannah's house? How had he and Hannah met?

Thought Questions
1. What does *doctrine* mean? Why do you think it was so important to the Puritans?
2. Was Aunt Rachel right that "evil can seem innocent and harmless"?
3. Do you agree that "children are evil by nature and that they have to be held with a firm hand"? Discuss.
4. What kind of person was Nat Eaton? How do you know?

Chapter 11

Review Questions
1. Why was Mercy so patient?
2. Who had left the flowers outside the dame school?
3. Where did Kit teach Prudence to read?
4. What invisible ingredient made Hannah's "cure" unfailing?
5. What did Kit discover while John was reading?

Thought Questions
1. Was learning to read valuable to the colonists? In what way?
2. Was it right for Kit to put Prudence at risk by taking her to see Hannah? Discuss.

Chapter 12

Review Questions
1. How did Kit realize that Aunt Rachel knew about her visits to Hannah?
2. To what did Nat compare Kit while they were working on the roof?
3. Why was Kit in trouble when she returned home?
4. What did Uncle Matthew forbid Kit to do?

Thought Questions
1. Why do you think the Puritans wanted life to be so solemn?
2. What is the purpose of education? Based on Nat's remarks to Kit, how would he answer?
3. Nat said, "There are two sides to loyalty"? Explain. Do you agree?
4. What is *treason*?

Chapter 13

Review Questions
1. What was a husking bee?
2. Why were red ears of corn significant?
3. Why did John warn Kit about associating with Hannah?
4. What did John reveal to Kit about his hopes?
5. How did Judith and Uncle Matthew misunderstand John's intentions?

Thought Questions
1. Do you think John was a coward for not correcting Judith's assumption? What does his choice tell you about his character?

Chapter 14

Review Questions

1. Describe autumn in New England.
2. What did Kit observe Uncle Matthew doing? Why did she think it was significant?
3. Why did Nat snub Kit when the *Dolphin* came?
4. What made Uncle Matthew late for dinner? What word had come from Sir Edmond Andros?

Chapter 15

Review Questions

1. Why was William among the men meeting with Uncle Matthew?
2. Describe Governor Andros and his escort.
3. What happened to the charter?

Thought Questions

1. Why were the men offended by the thought of swearing with their hand on the Bible? When did this practice become normal?
2. When Uncle Matthew found out the charter was safe, he said, "Then we can hold up our heads." Why was the charter so important?

Chapter 16

Review Questions

1. Why was there to be no Thanksgiving?
2. What happened on All Hallows' Eve?
3. How were the culprits punished?
4. What did Kit use to teach Prudence to read?
5. Why was John leaving Wethersfield?

Thought Questions

1. Hannah told Kit, "Thee has never escaped at all if love is not there." Explain.

Chapter 17

Review Questions

1. Who finally brought Dr. Bulkeley in to help Mercy when she was ill?
2. What method did Dr. Bulkeley use to cure Mercy?
3. Who burst into the house that night, after Dr. Bulkeley had left? What did they want Uncle Matthew to do?
4. What did Kit decide to do?
5. How did Hannah get away from Wethersfield?
6. What did Kit find when she returned home?

Thought Questions

1. The men said the accusation against Kit was "only women's talk." What does this phrase mean?
2. Why did Uncle Matthew condemn Hannah but not join in the witch hunt? What does this choice reveal about his character?

Chapter 18

Review Questions
1. What had made Uncle Matthew change his mind about Kit?
2. Who came to the door later that afternoon? What did they want?
3. How did Goodwife Cruff explain Hannah's disappearance?
4. What had the mob found at Hannah's house?
5. Why did the constable want to lock up Kit?
6. What had happened to the other women previously accused of witchcraft?
7. Who came to visit Kit that night?

Thought Questions
1. What do you think of the colony's system of justice? Do you think it was just? Why or why not?
2. Did it make a difference that Prudence could read when she was half-starved and beaten and overworked? Discuss.

Chapter 19

Review Questions
1. What did the constable's wife say would happen at the examination?
2. Of what was Kit accused?
3. What evidence did Goodman Cruff present?
4. Who arrived, bringing a new witness in the case?
5. Who was the new witness? What evidence did she present?
6. What persuaded Goodman Cruff to withdraw his charges?

Thought Questions
1. Where did the testimony against Kit come from? Were all the witnesses lying?
2. What standards of proof were used in this trial? Did the colonists believe someone was innocent until proven guilty?

Chapter 20

Review Questions
1. What news did William bring about John during the first snow?
2. Why did Kit tell William not to return?
3. Whose arrival interrupted Thankful Peabody's wedding?
4. What did Kit resolve that winter?
5. Who arrived at the house during the March blizzard?

Thought Questions
1. William had not come to save Kit at the trial. Why not? What does this tell you about his character?
2. Why did the Puritans not celebrate Christmas?

Chapter 21

Review Questions
1. Whose weddings were announced at the Lecture Day in April?
2. What did Kit plan to do with her elegant dresses?
3. What did Kit realize about her dream of returning to Barbados?
4. When Nat returned to Wethersfield, why did he not come on the *Dolphin*?

5. What had he named his new ship? In whose honor had he named it?
6. When did Nat say he would take Kit aboard?

Thought Questions

1. Kit said, "Nat is New England." What do you think she meant? What had New England come to mean to Kit?
2. What impression does *The Witch of Blackbird Pond* give you of the Puritans? Is it positive or negative?
3. Does this story have a moral? What does Speare's novel suggest about love, tolerance, compassion, and justice? Discuss.

Brain Work
ASKING A QUESTION

Imagine you were going to write a paper about *The Witch of Blackbird Pond*. Keeping in mind what you have learned about asking a good essay question, come up with a question that you might use to start an essay in each of the following categories.*

Example: Cultural attitudes – Why were the Puritans and the Quakers so antagonistic?

1. Plot –

2. Characters –

3. Themes –

4. Philosophy (of the characters or the narrator) –

5. Historical events –

Hint – use the Thought Questions to jump-start your ideas.

Johnny Tremain
Esther Forbes

Esther Forbes (1891-1967) grew up in New England, where she struggled in school because she was dyslexic and had poor eyesight. Nonetheless, she showed great talent for storytelling and creative writing. After working briefly for a publishing house, Forbes released her own first novel when she was thirty-five. She went on to write mainly about historical periods and figures like Paul Revere—a book that earned her a Pulitzer Prize in history. *Johnny Tremain*, a novel about a young man growing up in Boston at the start of the American Revolution, was published in 1943, and won the Newbery Medal in 1944.

Chapter 1 – Up and About

Review Questions
1. Why were Mr. Lapham's apprentices luckier than most?
2. Who was the boss of the house?
3. Why did Mr. Lapham assign Johnny the readings from Leviticus and Proverbs?
4. What did Mr. Hancock order?
5. What was the story behind Johnny's middle initial?

Thought Questions
1. Are people "made" for certain professions? How much of your skill is determined by God and how much is determined by your own efforts?
2. Johnny said the two elder Laphams would make good wives because they were big and buxom. How have our society's values changed? What makes a society change its values?
3. What are the benefits of the apprentice system? What are the disadvantages?
4. Mr. Lapham seemed to think piety and patriotism were mutually exclusive. What do you think?

Chapter 2 – The Pride of your Power

Review Questions
1. Whom did Johnny go to for advice about the silver basin?
2. What did the master silversmith offer Johnny?
3. What kept Johnny from finishing the basin? What happened to his hand?

Thought Questions
1. Do you think working on Sunday should be against the law? Defend your position.
2. When does leisure turn into boredom?
3. Why do you think Mr. Lapham believed Dove's claim of piety?

Chapter 3 – An Earth of Brass

Review Questions
1. What prevented Johnny from being hired?
2. What effect did Mr. Tweedie have on the Lapham household?
3. What did Johnny do with the money from Mr. Hancock?

Thought Questions
1. Johnny, "felt able to stand aside from his problems—see himself," when he met Rab. Explain.
2. What is the difference between arrogance and pride in one's work?
3. Why couldn't Mr. Hancock help giving Johnny the silver?
4. What made Isannah's cries "the worst thing anyone had said to [Johnny]?

Chapter 4 – The Rising Eye

Review Questions
1. How did Mr. Lyte respond to Johnny's claim?
2. What happened at the Lyte home?
3. Why did Mrs. Lapham refuse to let Cilla testify?
4. What was the result of the lawsuit?

Thought Questions
1. Why did Cilla's insults make Johnny feel better?
2. Does the death penalty seem like a harsh punishment for theft? Explain.

Chapter 5 – The Boston Observer

Review Questions
1. What did Johnny do with his cup?
2. Who hired Johnny? For what job?
3. What was wrong with Goblin?
4. Why did the loft in the printing shop have so many chairs?
5. What changed in Rab at the dance? What else happened there?

Thought Questions
1. Why did Johnny pattern his manners after Rab? Why do we mimic some people and not others?
2. Explain the quote, "he might have taken to crime—because that was what was expected of him."

3. Analyze the events at the butcher shop. What do they tell you about Rab's character? Johnny's?

Chapter 6 – Salt Water Tea

Review Questions
1. What tax was causing such a stir for the people of Boston?
2. What did Dr. Warren ask Johnny about his hand? How did they misunderstand each other?
3. What signal was Johnny to wait for at the meeting?
4. Who attempted to profit from the "tea party"?

Thought Questions
1. How is the Sabbath observed or protected today? Discuss.
2. Should Christianity be a matter for government? What would be the pros and cons?
3. Were the Sons of Liberty noble?
4. Why did the Sons of Liberty take care not to damage the other cargo?

Chapter 7 – The Fiddler's Bill

Review Questions
1. What was the fiddler's bill?
2. How did Johnny help the cause by carrying messages for the British?
3. Why did Cilla come to the Boston Observer? What had happened to Isannah?
4. How did Johnny trick Lieutenant Stranger?
5. Why did Rab and Johnny need Dove?
6. What would keep Cilla and Isannah safe in Milton?

Thought Questions
1. Is it wiser politically to stop sedition (press that calls for rebellion) or to allow it?
2. How did Cilla's changed attitude toward Johnny change his feelings for her?
3. Can children be "too young to be lascivious"? Discuss.

Chapter 8 – A World to Come

Review Questions
1. In what manner did the Lytes return to Boston?
2. What did Johnny find in Mr. Lyte's Bible? What did he do with it?
3. What happened when Rab tried to buy a gun?

Thought Questions
1. Why did Cilla go back for the silver?
2. Why couldn't Johnny think of the redcoats as targets?
3. Sam Adams said, "I will work for war" not peace. What is your reaction? Was peace possible?
4. According to James Otis, the revolution was "only that a man can stand up." Do you agree?

Chapter 9 – The Scarlet Deluge

Review Questions
1. Who were the leaders of the Boston Whigs?
2. What did Johnny learn from Lydia? From Dove?

3. Why did the soldiers stop Johnny? How did he escape? Who helped him?
4. What happened to Pumpkin?

Thought Questions
1. What do you think of Johnny's methods for getting information? Do "ends justify the means"?
2. Does the "shifting about" of roles between Johnny and Lieutenant Stranger seem odd to you?
3. Pumpkin said the British soldiers would fight, even those who hated the army. Why?

Chapter 10 – 'Disperse, Ye Rebels'

Review Questions
1. Why did Rab leave Boston?
2. What did Johnny learn from Dove?
3. Where and when did the war begin?

Thought Questions
1. Do you think Johnny's dream about the lobsters meant anything? If so, what?
2. Does deception become permissible in war time? Under what circumstances?

Chapter 11 – Yankee Doodle

Review Questions
1. Who won the battle of Lexington?
2. How did Uncle Lorne escape the soldiers?
3. What happened to Cilla and Isannah when the Lytes left Boston?
4. What did Lavinia tell Johnny?

Thought Questions
1. Why was Dr. Warren so sure that Americans would end the war?
2. It seemed right to Sergeant Gale that "men went to war and women wept." Have things changed?
3. How has the meaning of liberty changed since Johnny's time?
4. Is a 16-year old a child or an adult? Does it depend, as Johnny said, on the situation?

Chapter 12 - A Man Can Stand Up

Review Questions
1. Where did Johnny find Dr. Warren?
2. What did Rab ask Johnny to do? Why?
3. What did Dr. Warren tell Johnny about his hand?

Thought Questions
1. Do you think Johnny's response to the news about his hand was different than it would have been if he had found out earlier? If so, why?
2. What does this book suggest is more important: individuals, or the causes for which they fight? Do you agree?

Brain Work
DEVELOPING A THESIS

If you were writing about *Johnny Tremain*, you might ask a question like one of the questions listed below. For each sample question, try to come up with a thesis on which you could write a 2-3 page essay. Remember, you want to find middle ground between a thesis that is too obvious and one that is unsupportable: make sure you could support your thesis using evidence from the book.

> **Example**: Does Johnny ever truly lose his arrogance? ⇨ Through the course of the book, Johnny moves from pride in his work, to plain arrogance, and back to pride in work well done.

1. What is the main theme of *Johnny Tremain*?

2. What is Johnny's philosophy about honesty?

3. Does *Johnny Tremain* romanticize the American Revolution and the men who started it?

4. What does *Johnny Tremain* say about the system of apprenticeship?

The Call of the Wild
Jack London

John Griffith London (1876-1916) was born in California, but he traveled widely as a young man; among other short-lived careers, he spent time on a sealing ship and in the Yukon panning for gold. London, who preferred the name Jack, finally turned to writing as an alternative to a job doing manual labor. As a writer, he incorporated his experiences into his stories and travel narratives, but he was also deeply interested in social and political issues. *The Call of the Wild*, his best-known book, was published in 1903. In this book, London deals with the conditions of life in the Yukon during the gold rush, but he also explores questions of nature, philosophy, and social behavior.

Chapter 1 – Into the Primitive

Review Questions
1. Why was trouble brewing for Buck?
2. How did that trouble manifest itself?
3. How did the man with the red sweater break Buck?
4. What did the club teach Buck?
5. Who bought Buck?

Thought Questions
1. The book opens with a four-line poem. How does this poem relate to the rest of the book?
2. What is the reign of primitive law?
3. Is it ever present among humans?

Chapter 2 – The Law of Club and Fang

Review Questions
1. What happened to Curly?
2. What was Buck's new job?
3. What marked Buck fit to survive in the hostile Northland?

   4. What did Buck relearn from his instincts?

Thought Questions
   1. What was the law of club and fang?
   2. Did Buck have a natural reason to fear traps, or was it only "harkening back…to the lives of his forebears"?
   3. London calls the moral nature a "vain thing" and a "handicap." Do you agree? Defend your answer.
   4. London defines civilization by opposites as, "doing what is right instead of what is easy." How would you define *civilization*?

Chapter 3 – The Dominant Primordial Beast

Review Questions
   1. Who was Buck's greatest enemy and rival?
   2. What triggered their fight?
   3. What ended it?
   4. What did François make for Buck?
   5. What happened to Dolly?
   6. What activity did Buck share with the other dogs in Dawson?
   7. What started the final fight between Spitz and Buck?
   8. What quality allowed Buck to win?

Thought Questions
   1. Do people have a pride that is comparable to the "pride of trail and trace"? What is it?
   2. Why did the dogs' songs stir Buck so deeply?
   3. London compares Buck's blood lust to that of men hunting. Do you agree?

Chapter 4 – Who has Won to Mastership

Review Questions
   1. Why did Buck refuse to take his old place in the traces?
   2. Who took over the team from François and Perrault?
   3. From where did Buck's most potent memories come?
   4. What did Buck dream?
   5. What happened to Dave?

Thought Questions
   1. Was Buck's leadership really any different from Spitz's?
   2. Can a dog be homesick? Why or why not?
   3. What did Buck's dream mean? Suggest a possible interpretation.

Chapter 5 – The Toil of Trace and Trail

Review Questions
   1. What orders awaited the tired dogs at Skagway?
   2. Who bought the dogs?
   3. Why couldn't the dogs start the sled?
   4. What did Charles and Hal miscalculate in their planning?
   5. What advice did John Thornton give Hal?
   6. Why did Buck change owners?

7. What happened to the rest of the team?

Thought Questions
1. Why do you think some people developed the "patience of the trail" and not others?
2. Why did Thornton pity Buck more than the other dogs?

Chapter 6 – For the Love of a Man

Review Questions
1. Why had Thornton stopped short of Dawson?
2. What did Buck experience for the first time with Thornton and his dogs?
3. What did Buck fear?
4. What called Buck away from the camp?
5. What drew him back?
6. How did Buck save Thornton's life?
7. What wager did Thornton make about Buck?
8. What was the outcome?

Thought Questions
1. Was Buck a civilized dog or a thing of the wild at heart?
2. For humans, is there a middle course between mastery and being mastered?
3. Do you think mercy ever exists in primordial life? Defend your position.

Chapter 7 – The Sounding of the Call

Review Questions
1. What did Thornton set out to find?
2. What did he and his partners find?
3. What did Buck pursue in the woods? Why?
4. Why did Buck challenge the bull moose?
5. What awaited Buck when he returned to the camp?
6. Why did Buck finally obey the call of the wild?
7. What was Buck's new life?

Thought Questions
1. What makes an animal a killer?
2. What makes a human a killer?
3. In your opinion, would the wildness in Buck have come out if he had been left with Judge Miller?
4. Do you accept London's claim that a primordial urge lingers in all creatures? Why or why not?

Hand Work
REVISING THE CONCLUSION

Imagine you are writing an essay about *The Call of the Wild*. The topic of your paper is a comparison of Buck's relationships with Judge Miller and John Thornton. Your thesis and outline are below. For practice, write a one-paragraph conclusion based on what you think the paper would look like.

Thesis: Buck's relationship with John Thornton is a combination of his relationship with Judge Miller and his experiences in the wilderness.

Outline:
I. Buck's relationship with Judge Miller
1. Affection
2. Loyalty
3. Pride

II. Buck's experiences in the wilderness
1. Independence

III. Buck's relationship with John Thornton
1. Affection
2. Loyalty
3. Pride
4. Independence

Remember, your conclusion should wrap up the most important points, summarize the argument for your thesis, and close with a memorable thought about the broader implications of what you have to say. Since you are not actually writing the full essay, focus on the most important parts. What would you need to demonstrate in order to prove the thesis? What lasting thought would you want to leave with readers? You can use either a quote or a statement as your memorable thought, as long as it is closely related to the thesis.

The Adventures of Tom Sawyer
Mark Twain

Samuel Langhorne Clemens (1835-1910), the name of a Missouri-born newspaper assistant, is not a familiar name in American literature. Mark Twain, on the other hand, is legendary. After working in several aspects of newspaper publishing, when he was twenty-three, Clemens became a licensed river pilot and took on the pen name Mark Twain, a river term referring to a safe depth of water (two fathoms deep). During his career, Twain wrote both short stories and novels about a range of subjects, but his most famous works are based on life along the Mississippi River. *The Adventures of Tom Sawyer*, one of his best-known novels, was published in 1876.

Chapter 1

Review Questions
1. How did Tom evade his aunt?
2. How did Aunt Polly discover Tom had "played hookey"?
3. Why did Tom and the new boy fight?

Thought Questions
1. Aunt Polly believed, "spare the rod and spile [sic] the child." What do you think?
2. If, as Twain says, new enterprises make men forget their troubles, are inventors always happy?

Chapter 2

Review Questions
1. What was Tom's punishment for fighting?
2. How did Tom trick the other boys?

Thought Questions
1. Is it a law of human action that we covet what is difficult for us to attain?
2. What is your definition of work? Of play?

Chapter 3

Review Questions
1. What did the new girl give Tom?
2. Who broke the sugar bowl? Who was punished for it?
3. What happened to Tom at the new girl's house?

Thought Questions
1. How were Tom's infatuations different from ones teenagers have today?
2. What do you think of Aunt Polly's discipline? Her parenting skills?

Chapter 4

Review Questions
1. What did Mary give Tom? Why did she give it to him?
2. Why did Tom trade for the colored tickets?
3. How did Tom manage to sit with the new girl?

Thought Questions
1. When does a talent become "showing off"?

Chapter 5

Review Questions
1. What tormented Tom during the prayer?
2. What happened to Tom's beetle?

Thought Questions
1. The boys were tired of having Willie Mufferson "thrown up to them." What did they mean?
2. "The less there is to justify a traditional custom, the harder it is to get rid of it." Do you agree?

Chapter 6

Review Questions
1. Why did Tom hate Mondays?
2. Why was Huckleberry Finn hated by the mothers of the town?
3. Why did Tom make the schoolmaster angry?

Thought Questions
1. Where do children learn superstitions? How are superstitions spread?
2. What makes something valuable?

Chapter 7

Review Questions
1. How did Tom and Joe amuse themselves?
2. How did Tom spoil his engagement?

Thought Questions
1. What did engagement mean to Tom? What does it mean today?

Chapter 8

Review Questions
1. What career did Tom choose?
2. What was Tom's "structure of faith"? Why did it fail him?

Thought Questions
1. What did Tom mean when he wished to die temporarily?
2. Why do outlaws and pirates have such charm for children?

Chapter 9

Review Questions
1. Whom did Tom sneak out with that night?
2. Who were the "devils" Tom and his friend saw? Why had they come?
3. What did the boys witness?

Thought Questions
1. Why do you think Tom felt the need to talk in the graveyard?

Chapter 10

Review Questions
1. What did the boys decide to do about what they had seen?
2. Whom did the boys find with the hogs?
3. What was the final blow to Tom (at school)?

Thought Questions
1. Did the boys make the right choice? Can you understand their reasons?
2. Why is a rebuke sometimes worse than a whipping?

Chapter 11

Review Questions
1. Was the murderer caught?
2. What made Sid suspicious of Tom?
3. What did Tom do at the jail?

Chapter 12

Review Questions
1. What distracted Tom from the murder case?
2. What cure broke through Tom's indifference?
3. How did Becky respond when she saw Tom at school?

Thought Questions
1. Why hadn't Aunt Polly realized "what was cruelty to a cat might be cruelty to a boy, too"?

Chapter 13

Review Questions
1. Why was Joe running away?
2. What did the boys decide to become?

   3. Where did they set up camp?

Thought Questions
   1. How does Tom's logic for choosing a life of crime compare to that of real criminals?
   2. What is a conscience?
   3. Can a pirate NOT steal?

Chapter 14

Review Questions
   1. What ailed the boys after they finished exploring the island?
   2. What did the boys hear?
   3. Who first suggested going home?

Thought Questions
   1. What is *homesickness*? Why are some people affected more strongly than others?

Chapter 15

Review Questions
   1. Who was with Aunt Polly?
   2. What did Tom hear?
   3. Were Huck and Joe glad to have Tom back?

Thought Questions
   1. Why do you think Tom returned to the town?

Chapter 16

Review Questions
   1. Who wanted to leave the camp?
   2. What did Huck teach the boys to do?
   3. What had the boys failed to prepare for?

Chapter 17

Review Questions
   1. How did the townsfolk talk about the missing boys in their absence?
   2. What disturbed the funeral service?

Thought Questions
   1. What do you think expressed the most affection, cuffs or kisses?

Chapter 18

Review Questions
   1. What "dream" did Tom tell Aunt Polly?
   2. What did the adventure do for Tom's popularity?

Thought Questions
   1. Was Tom and Becky's fighting any more foolish than teenagers' is today?

Chapter 19

Review Questions
1. What did Aunt Polly learn from Mrs. Harper?
2. How did Tom soothe her?

Thought Questions
1. Is there such a thing as a "good lie"?

Chapter 20

Review Questions
1. What did Becky do that deserved whipping?
2. Was she whipped for it?

Chapter 21

Review Questions
1. What did the schoolboys do to Mr. Dobbins?

Thought Questions
1. According to Twain, girls always end compositions with a sermon. Is this true? Why would he think that?

Chapter 22

Review Questions
1. Who were the Cadets of Temperance?
2. Did the Revival spirit last? If not, why not?

Thought Questions
1. Do you agree with the principle that we want to do what we promise not to do?

Chapter 23

Review Questions
1. Who was a surprise witness for the defense in Muff's trial?
2. What was the outcome of the trial?

Thought Questions
1. If Muff were guilty, do you agree it would be "right and best" for him to be hanged?
2. Did Muff get a fair trial? Explain.

Chapter 24

Thought Questions
1. Are people as fickle in real life as the townspeople were in their opinions of Muff?

Chapter 25

Review Questions
1. What desire came over Tom?
2. What did Tom plan to do with his share of the money?

Thought Questions
1. Why do kings only have a given name?

Chapter 26

Review Questions
1. What did the boys find at the haunted house?
2. Who was the Spaniard?
3. What did the men uncover?
4. How did the men realize the boys had been there?

Thought Questions
1. Do greed and revenge come from the same emotion? Does a common emotion inspire other sins?

Chapter 27

Review Questions
1. What did Huck want to do about the money?
2. What was Tom's plan?

Thought Questions
1. "[Tom] did not care to have Huck's company in public places." Explain.

Chapter 28

Review Questions
1. Whom did Tom see in the tavern room?
2. How did the boys explain the haunted room?

Chapter 29

Review Questions
1. When Huck followed Injun Joe, where did they end up?
2. What did Injun Joe plan to do? How did Huck respond?

Thought Questions
1. Injun Joe said, "When you want to get revenge on a woman…you go for her looks." Is this true? Why or why not?

Chapter 30

Review Questions
1. Had the Welshman caught or killed Injun Joe and his friend?
2. What had happened to Tom and Becky?
3. Who took care of Huck?

Chapter 31

Review Questions
1. How did Becky lose her candle?
2. What did Tom and Becky eat in the cave?

3. Whom did Tom meet in the cave?

Chapter 32

Review Questions
1. When were the children found?
2. How had they escaped?
3. What did the judge tell Tom, and why did it upset him?

Chapter 33

Review Questions
1. What did the men find in the cave?
2. Where was the money, according to Tom?
3. What new career did the cave inspire Tom to pursue?

Thought Questions
1. Does everything have a purpose and a mission?
2. Why do you think some townspeople were petitioning for Injun Joe's pardon?

Chapter 34

Review Questions
1. Why were Huck and Tom taken to the widow's house?
2. How did Tom break up the party?

Chapter 35

Review Questions
1. Did Huck enjoy his new life? How do you know?
2. What did Huck ask Tom to do? How did Tom convince him to change his mind?

Thought Questions
1. How does Tom and Huck's treatment compare to the way celebrities are treated today?
2. What are the pros and cons of being rich?

Brain Work
BUILDING AN ARGUMENT

Remember, when you build an argument, your reader should be able to follow each step in your line of reasoning without having to make leaps in logic. Two sample theses on *Tom Sawyer* are listed below. For each thesis, write out the steps you would need to follow in order to prove your point. Make sure every point follows logically from the last.

1. The portrayal of non-white races in *Tom Sawyer* was influenced by the culture of the time it was written.

2. Aunt Polly's methods of discipline were a result of Tom's actions, rather than the other way around.

An Old-Fashioned Girl
Louisa May Alcott

Louisa May Alcott (1832-1888) was born in Pennsylvania, where her father, Bronson Alcott, was a prominent philosopher. In an effort to support her family, Alcott worked a variety of jobs and also found time to write extensively. She began by publishing short stories, poetry, and sketches, but her most popular works are those she wrote in response to a request to write something for young girls. In 1868, using her childhood experiences growing up with three sisters, Alcott wrote *Little Women*, a novel set during the Civil War. She went on to write several other successful and popular novels for young women. *An Old-Fashioned Girl*, about a country girl trying to fit into city life and yet stay true to herself, was published in 1870.

Chapter 1 – Polly Arrives

Review Questions
1. Why didn't Fanny want to go to the station?
2. How had Fanny described Tom?
3. Why did Tom treat Polly badly on the way home? How did he fool her?
4. Why did Madam like Polly so much?
5. What made Polly uncomfortable at the theater?

Thought Questions
1. Are any characteristics common to all brother-sister relationships? If so, what are they?
2. Is good English fashionable today? Why or why not?
3. Is it easy to "get used to" temptations? What makes it harder or easier?

Chapter 2 – New Fashions

Review Questions
1. Why was Carrie's scandal inconvenient for Fanny and her friends?
2. What did the young ladies do at recess?
3. What did Fanny ask Polly to keep secret?
4. Who surprised Fanny and Polly on the way home from the concert?
5. How did Tom ruin the first batch of candy? What happened to the second batch?

Thought Questions
1. Did Fanny lie to her mother? Defend your answer.
2. Polly said, "A real gentleman is as polite to a little girl as to a woman." Do you agree? What marks a true gentleman today? Is the term "gentleman" still used? Why or why not?

Chapter 3 – Polly's Troubles

Review Questions
1. How did Polly and Maud interact? Polly and Tom?
2. Why did grandma and Polly get along so well? Grandma and Tom?
3. What did Polly do with the little girls (and Tom) one afternoon? How did the family find out?
4. What did Fanny suggest that bothered Polly?
5. To what temptation did Polly yield?

Thought Questions
1. Was it improper for Polly to go coasting? Why? What makes something proper or improper?
2. Alcott describes "little people playing at love" as the silliest activity of all. Do you agree?
3. Is flirting wrong by its very nature? Explain.

Chapter 4 – Little Things

Review Questions
1. What "play" did Polly devise for Maud?
2. How did Polly show affection for Mr. Shaw?
3. With what did Polly help Tom? How did he help her?
4. What did Tom want from his father? What had he done to earn it?
5. How did Polly prove her courage to Tom?

Thought Questions
1. Is it more important to find the cause of unhappiness or to fix it? Explain.
2. Does being good come more easily to some people than to others? Discuss.

Chapter 5 – Scrapes

Review Questions
1. What was "Polly's stupidity"?
2. What did Tom ask Polly to do? What happened when she refused?
3. How did Maud get into trouble?

Thought Questions
1. Is it as bad to let someone believe something that is false as it is to tell a lie?
2. Which is more important: keeping promises or telling the truth? Defend your answer.

Chapter 6 – Grandma

Review Questions
1. Where was Polly? What was she doing with grandma?
2. What did the phrase "purple stockings" mean to grandma?

3. In Tom's story, how had the robber's mark gotten on grandma's door?
4. Why was the glove Polly chose so special?
5. Why did Fanny and Polly quarrel?

Thought Questions
1. Compare Polly to the young lady (Anne Boleyn) in the first letter of grandma's. How were they the same? How were they different?
2. Do you think Polly's mother preached? If not, what is the difference?

Chapter 7 – Goodbye

Review Questions
1. Why wasn't Polly happy before her farewell party?
2. Who danced the first number with Polly?
3. How did Polly settle the argument between Maud and her friends?
4. Why, according to Polly, should she not go to many parties?
5. What was Tom's goodbye present?

Thought Questions
1. How have social expectations for young men and women changed? What is now expected?
2. Is it better to work through envy or to avoid the things that cause it?

Chapter 8 – Six Years Afterward

Review Questions
1. What were Polly's winter plans?
2. How had Tom changed, and why was Polly disappointed in him?
3. What had Polly learned from the Shaws?
4. Who was Tom's fiancée?
5. Why did Polly say poverty would be good for Fanny?

Thought Questions
1. What makes someone beautiful or handsome? Is there any one characteristic that does?
2. How do you think an engaged person should look/act?

Chapter 9 – Lessons

Review Questions
1. What did Polly discover about being a working woman?
2. Whose snub hurt Polly most?
3. What project of Miss Mills' cheered Polly and made her forget her troubles?

Thought Questions
1. Is a big sacrifice or a small daily one harder, in your opinion? Why?
2. What is your response when you meet someone whose trials are greater than your own?

Chapter 10 – Brothers and Sisters

Review Questions
1. Why was Sunday Polly's happiest day?

   2. Why was Maud neglected?
   3. What is a public admonition? Why did Maud want to know?
   4. How had Tom helped Will?

Thought Questions
   1. What home influences are most important to you?
   2. Is "painting" (makeup) a big deal today? Why do people use it?
   3. How are persuasive influences different from moralizing?

Chapter 11 – Needles and Tongues

Review Questions
   1. What did Fanny ask Polly to do? Why was she reluctant?
   2. Why did Trix especially dislike Polly?
   3. What did Polly suggest the girls could do?
   4. What did the girls do for Jane?

Thought Questions
   1. Are women's rights activists looked down on today? If so, why?
   2. Does fashionable life "drill the character out of [young people]"? How?
   3. Can there be too much charity? Explain.

Chapter 12 – Forbidden Fruit

Review Questions
   1. What did Fanny invite Polly to do?
   2. Who met the threesome at the opera? Why wasn't Trix there?
   3. Why, according to Polly, did Clara Bird look tired?
   4. What happened as a result of Polly's excursion?

Thought Questions
   1. Why do you think Alcott included the aside to the reader about Young America and the English?
   2. "Dress plays a very important part in the lives of most women." Do you agree?
   3. How does dress interpret individual taste and character?

Chapter 13 – The Sunny Side

Review Questions
   1. What wager had Fanny won?
   2. What had Tom noticed about Polly? What did he suspect?
   3. What was Fanny's secret?
   4. What was Becky sculpting?

Thought Questions
   1. What does strong-minded mean? Is it a bad thing?
   2. Do women still pay the price for money and success? How is it different now?

Chapter 14 – Nipped in the Bud

Review Questions
   1. What did Polly feel that she must do? Why?
   2. What was Polly's "delicate and dangerous task"?

   3. Who interrupted Polly's stroll in the park?

   4. What mistake did Polly make in her intended message? What was the result?

Chapter 15 – Breakers Ahead

Review Questions

   1. What was wrong with Tom? What did he ask Polly to do? What was her response?

   2. What had happened to Mr. Shaw?

   3. Why was Fanny glad at the news?

   4. What friend did Polly mean "would be kinder than ever"?

Thought Questions

   1. Was Tom a coward? Why or why not?

   2. What is a *helpmeet*?

Chapter 16 – A Dress Parade

Review Questions

   1. How did the Shaws' friends demonstrate their caring?

   2. How did Maud handle bankruptcy?

   3. With what did Fanny ask Polly for assistance?

   4. What had Belle offered?

   5. What did Maud plan to do when she grew up?

Thought Questions

   1. What debts did Polly need to repay to the Shaws?

   2. "Blessing, like curses, come home to rest." Is this always true?

Chapter 17 – Playing Grandmother

Review Questions

   1. Who was hit the hardest by the failure?

   2. "Why are bad boys like cake"?

   3. What two letters had Tom received?

   4. What did Tom ask Polly to do? What was his plan?

   5. Why did Polly find "playing grandmother" dangerous?

Thought Questions

   1. Does kindness knock worse than cruelty? If so, why?

   2. Is human nature the same in men and women? To what extent? How is it different?

Chapter 18 – The Woman Who Did Not Dare

Review Questions

   1. Why did Polly, Sydney, Fanny, and Tom become closer right before Tom left?

   2. What was wrong with Polly that autumn?

   3. What prevented Polly and Fanny from becoming sisters?

   4. Who was the first to become engaged?

Thought Questions

   1. Do men and women always communicate differently? Why? In what way?

   2. What is the difference between the women who dare and the women who stand and wait?

Chapter 19 – Tom's Success

Review Questions
1. How had Tom changed when he returned?
2. Who was the next to become engaged?
3. Whom did Tom love? What token of his love had he kept?
4. What happened to Maud? To Will?

Thought Questions
1. Why did Alcott include a side note about happy endings? Do you prefer happy endings? Why?
2. Are love and labor old-fashioned? Explain.

Hand Work
CHOOSING A TITLE

For each of the following sample theses of a paper about *An Old-Fashioned Girl*, choose a catchy title that a) informs the reader about the topic of the essay, and b) inspires the reader to want to know more. Make sure you understand what each thesis is trying to prove. Writing a brief outline for each thesis may help you get started. Try to get a feeling for the tone of the essay that might develop, and then attempt to incorporate that tone into your title.

1. In *An Old-Fashioned Girl*, Polly was not an inherently good person, but her flaws were under-emphasized by Alcott in an attempt to show contrast among the characters.

2. There is good reason to suspect that Polly, the main character in *An Old-Fashioned Girl*, could have come from a Christian family, or at least a family that followed Christian principles.

3. At its core, *An Old-Fashioned Girl* is about the struggle of women to find a meaningful place in a society where their worth as individuals was not generally recognized.

Billy Budd
Herman Melville

Herman Melville (1819-1891) was born in New York into the family of a wealthy merchant. Melville went on to pursue a career as a sailor, following in his family's legacy. His early writing consists mainly of travel narratives about his adventures and experiences in the South Seas. When he returned to New England, Melville became close friends with fellow writer Nathaniel Hawthorne. When he published *Moby Dick*, the whaling novel now considered his greatest work, in 1851, Melville dedicated the book to Hawthorne. *Billy Budd*, a novella, was written in the late 1800s, but the story was not published until 1924, after Melville's death. Also drawn from Melville's experiences as a sailor, *Billy Budd* asks challenging questions about the nature of justice.

Chapter 1

Review Questions
1. Who was the "Handsome Sailor"?
2. How did Billy enter the King's Service?

Thought Questions
1. Does a moral nature often coexist with strength and beauty?
2. Does impressment seem like an effective method for getting sailors? Why or why not?

Chapter 2

Review Questions
1. Was Billy intelligent?
2. What was his one flaw?

Thought Questions
1. Is vice worse if it stems from viciousness or from exuberance?
2. Are virtues natural?

Chapter 3

Review Questions

    1. What had happened in May 1797? What effect did it have on the story?

Thought Questions
    1. Why is the flag so heavily symbolic?
    2. Why do countries try to conceal records of their defeats or embarrassments?

Chapter 4

Review Questions
    1. What was Melville's "bypath"?
    2. How did inventiveness change sea warfare?
    3. Why is "personal prudence...no special virtue in a military man"?

Chapter 5

Review Questions
    1. What grievances were not addressed after the mutiny?

Chapter 6

Review Questions
    1. Who was captain of Billy's ship? What was his nickname?

Chapter 7

Review Questions
    1. What was Vere's favorite pastime?
    2. How did he relate to the other officers?

Thought Questions
    1. Do you have positive convictions? What are they?

Chapter 8

Review Questions
    1. Which petty officer was introduced? What was his role?
    2. What rumors surrounded him?

Chapter 9

Review Questions
    1. What produced such strict attention to duty in Billy?
    2. What kind of trouble did Billy get into?
    3. What did the Dansker call Billy? How did he explain Billy's problem?

Chapter 10

Review Questions
    1. What happened when Billy spilled his soup?
    2. How did Billy interpret the incident? What suggested that he was mistaken?

Chapter 11

Review Questions
1. Did Claggart have a good reason to dislike Billy?
2. How did Melville characterize Claggart's nature?

Thought Questions
1. Is it different to know the world and to know human nature?
2. Is there such a thing as natural depravity?

Chapter 12

Review Questions
1. How did Billy and Claggart compare physically?
2. For what did Claggart envy Billy?

Chapter 13

Review Questions
1. What had the spilled soup meant to Claggart?
2. Who was Squeak? How did he make the situation worse?

Thought Questions
1. "Consciences are unlike as foreheads." Explain. Do you agree?
2. What kind of people "can really form no conception of an unreciprocated malice"? Why?

Chapter 14

Review Questions
1. What is the weakness of a good nature?
2. What did the afterguard ask Billy? How did Billy respond?

Chapter 15

Review Questions
1. What did Billy wonder about the incident?
2. How did the afterguardsman behave toward Billy after that night?
3. Why didn't Billy tell the captain about the request?
4. How did Dansker interpret the events? Why did he call the afterguardsman a "cat's paw"?

Chapter 16

Review Questions
1. Why didn't Billy want to blame Claggart?

Thought Questions
1. Does innocence always decrease as intelligence increases?
2. Can good people have an intuitive knowledge of the bad?

Chapter 17

Review Questions

1. Explain Claggart's different reactions to Billy.
2. Why did the Armourer and Captain of the Hold show dislike for Billy?

Thought Questions
1. What is a "too fair-spoken man"?

Chapter 18

Review Questions
1. Why was the *Bellipotent 74* (or *Indomitable*, in some versions) used for scouting missions?
2. Why did Claggart want to see Captain Vere? How did the captain respond to the news?
3. How did Vere "test the accuser"?

Chapter 19

Review Questions
1. What did the captain ask Claggart to do?
2. How did Billy defend himself?
3. What was the "divine judgment on Ananias"?

Thought Questions
1. Was it the captain's fault that Billy did what he did? Defend your answer.

Chapter 20

Review Questions
1. What did the surgeon believe Captain Vere should do?
2. Why was the surgeon unable to do anything about the situation?

Thought Questions
1. What do you think Captain Vere should have done in that situation?

Chapter 21

Review Questions
1. Who was the victim in legal terms?
2. Why did Captain Vere want to avoid publicity? Why did he have a sense of urgency?
3. How did Billy defend himself to the court? What question made him hesitate? Why?
4. Why, according to Vere, could they not "convict and yet mitigate the penalty"?
5. What was the court's decision?

Thought Questions
1. Where would you draw the line between sanity and insanity?
2. In terms of "essential right and wrong," who do you think was guilty?
3. Was this a clash of military duty and moral scruple? If so, which should have won?
4. Vere said, "The heart is the feminine in man." Discuss.
5. "It is easy for a non-combatant to reason about how [a battle] ought to have been fought. It is another thing personally and under fire to direct the fight." Is this an excuse for poor decisions?

Chapter 22

Review Questions
1. Who relayed to Billy the court's decision?

Chapter 23

Review Questions
1. How did the crew respond to Vere's announcement?

Chapter 24

Review Questions
1. Why did the Chaplain leave Billy without speaking to him on his first visit?
2. How did Billy view death?
3. How did Billy respond to the Chaplain's offers of Christianity?

Thought Questions
1. Is innocence better than religion to take to judgment? Was Billy innocent?
2. Do you agree with Melville that Chaplaincy is an absurd concept? Why or why not?

Chapter 25

Review Questions
1. Why was Billy hanged on the main-yard?
2. What did Billy say before he died?

Thought Questions
1. Some of Melville's language makes a biblical comparison between Billy and Jesus. Find an example. Do you think *Billy Budd* could be an allegory for Christ's life and death? Explain.

Chapter 26

Review Questions
1. What was unusual about Billy's death? How did the surgeon explain it?

Chapter 27

Review Questions
1. What triggered the sailors' superstitions?
2. Why did Vere disrupt the sailors' normal routine?

Chapter 28

Review Questions
1. How did Vere die?
2. What did he say before he died?

Thought Questions
1. Why was *Athée* (*Athéiste*, in some versions) the most apt name given to a war-ship?
2. Do you think Vere regretted sentencing Billy to death?

Chapter 29

Review Questions
1. What news appeared in the naval chronicle? How was the story altered?

Chapter 30

Review Question
1. Who wrote the ballad in Billy's honor?

Thought Questions
1. Why did the bluejackets follow the spar on which Billy had died? Melville said, "To them a chip of it was as a piece of the Cross." What was Melville trying to prove? Did he succeed?
2. According to Melville, the sailors had a deeper impression of Billy's innocence since he was gone. Why is it easier to remember the good qualities of those who are not present?

Brain Work
PREPARING AN OUTLINE

Once you have the step-by-step process for proving your thesis, the next logical step is to turn that mental path into an outline. Typically, you could organize a paper multiple ways. Two important considerations in choosing your organization are the logical progression of ideas and the emphasis you want to place on major points.

Each of the two theses listed below has two suggested outlines. Choose one for each thesis, and be able to explain why you chose that outline. Think about the logical order of the essay. If you're having a hard time, practice writing transitions for each outline; this should make your choice easier.

Thesis 1: Billy Budd caused the fall of Claggart as much as Claggart caused the fall of Billy.

Outline 1a.
   I.   Their characters were both upstanding before they met
   II. They both triggered each other's weaknesses (Claggart, inferiority; Billy, speechlessness)
   III. Both of their characters were compromised by the incident (Claggart, liar; Billy, killer)

Outline 1b.
   I.   Billy made Claggart feel inferior just as Claggart made Billy feel helpless and speechless
   II. Claggart was a good sailor just as Billy was a good sailor
   III. Both Claggart and Billy behaved immorally

Thesis 2: *Billy Budd* is an allegory for the Garden of Eden story.

Outline 2a.
   I.   Billy fell into immoral behavior (sin) after he met Claggart
   II. Billy had formerly been innocent, like Adam and Eve
   III. Claggart was sneaky and deceptive like Satan

Outline 2b.
   I.   Billy Budd was innocent like Adam and Eve
   II. Claggart was sneaky and deceptive like Satan
   III. Billy fell into immoral behavior because of Claggart, like Adam and Eve because of the serpent

The Scarlet Letter
Nathaniel Hawthorne

Nathaniel Hawthorne (1804-1864) was born in Salem, Massachusetts, and spent most of his youth in Salem or other parts of New England, where he also started his own newspaper. He was a friend of Herman Melville and other literary figures in the area, including the Alcotts, Thoreau, and Emerson. Much of Hawthorne's writing is tied to the local history of New England. In particular, because Hawthorne's great-grandfather was a judge in the Salem witch trials, many of Hawthorne's short stories revisit this period in history to consider the ethical dilemmas it poses. *The Scarlet Letter*, published in 1850, deals with similar issues. This novel examines the effects of sin in Puritan society.

Chapter 1 – The Prison Door

Review Questions
1. What two things were constant in every new colony?
2. What did the rose symbolize?

Chapter 2 – The Market-Place

Review Questions
1. How did the gossips think the case should have been handled?
2. What was Mistress Prynne's punishment?
3. Who was the misshapen scholar in Hester's vision?

Thought Questions
1. The Puritans were "A people amongst whom religion and law were almost identical."
   How closely do you think religion and law should be related? Why?
2. Is ridicule a crueler punishment than death? Explain.

Chapter 3 – The Recognition

Review Questions
1. Who was the stranger?
2. For what was Hester Prynne punished?
3. What did Reverend Wilson want Reverend Dimmesdale to do?

Thought Questions
1. Why did Hester consider public censure better than a personal confrontation? Do you agree?
2. Is "open ignominy" better or worse than "a guilty heart through life"? Why?

Chapter 4 – The Interview

Review Questions
1. Why did the jailer call a doctor?
2. Whom did he call?
3. Whom did Chillingworth blame for Hester's sin?
4. What did he ask her to reveal?
5. Why didn't Chillingworth want his identity known?

Chapter 5 – Hester at Her Needle

Review Questions
1. Why did Hester stay in the community?
2. By what art did Hester make a living?
3. What item was she not called upon to make?
4. Why did she dread children?

Thought Questions
1. Why was the daily struggle harder than the public humiliation?
2. "Giving up her individuality, she would become the general symbol at which the preacher and moralist might point." Why? Does this still happen?
3. Was Hester the only sinful person in the community? Explain.

Chapter 6 – Pearl

Review Questions
1. Why did Hester name her daughter Pearl?
2. Why couldn't Pearl follow rules?
3. What was unusual about her?
4. Who were Pearl's companions?
5. How did the townspeople explain her parentage?

Thought Questions
1. Can evil deeds have good results? Under what circumstances?
2. Can a parent's morality or lack thereof be passed on to a child? Why or why not?
3. What is your impression of Pearl?
4. Why was she fascinated with the scarlet letter?

Chapter 7 – The Governor's Hall

Review Questions

1. Why did Hester seek Governor Bellingham?
2. What was "the scarlet letter in another form"?
3. What prevented the town children from throwing mud at Hester and Pearl?

Thought Questions
1. How can something be an object of affection and an emblem of guilt at the same time?
2. Is it symbolic that Pearl, the "living scarlet letter," chased away Hester's tormenters? Discuss.

Chapter 8 – The Elf-Child and the Minister

Review Questions
1. Who were the governor's companions?
2. What did the governor suggest to Hester?
3. How did she respond?
4. Did Pearl support her mother's case? Explain.
5. Who spoke up for Hester?

Thought Questions
1. Is it wrong for ministers to enjoy and seek comfort?
2. When does it become hypocritical?
3. What do you think the scarlet letter taught Hester?
4. Do you agree with Mr. Dimmesdale's explanation of Pearl's purpose? Why or why not?
5. Did Hester need Pearl?
6. Did Pearl need Hester?

Chapter 9 – The Leech

Review Questions
1. Why was Chillingworth welcomed into the community so quickly?
2. What was the relationship between Chillingworth and Dimmesdale?
3. Why did some of the townspeople suspect Chillingworth?
4. Of what did they suspect him?

Thought Questions
1. Are doctors and scientists less likely to be spiritual?
2. Hawthorne says the "intricacies of that wondrous mechanism" (the human body and brain) cause men to lose their spiritual view of existence. Do you agree? Why or why not?
3. Is faith confining? Explain.

Chapter 10 – The Leech and His Patient

Review Questions
1. What was Roger Chillingworth investigating?
2. What did he hope to find?
3. Why, according to Dimmesdale, do some people keep their guilty secrets?
4. How did Chillingworth explain Dimmesdale's illness?

Thought Questions
1. "Trusting no man as his friend, he could not recognize his enemy." Do you agree?

  2. Is it always a relief to confess sin? Why or why not?

  3. What do you think Chillingworth saw on Dimmesdale's heart?

Chapter 11 – The Interior of a Heart

Review Questions

  1. How did Chillingworth and Dimmesdale's relationship change?

  2. Why was Dimmesdale so popular?

  3. What is a *scourge*? Why did Dimmesdale have one?

Thought Questions

  1. What "other sin" did Dimmesdale add by vaguely confessing to his congregation?

Chapter 12 – The Minister's Vigil

Review Questions

  1. Where did Dimmesdale go?

  2. Who interrupted his vigil?

  3. What did he ask Hester and Pearl to do?

  4. What did Pearl ask in return?

  5. How were they revealed? To whom?

Thought Questions

  1. "Crime is for the iron-nerved." Explain. Do you agree?

  2. Why wouldn't Dimmesdale stand with Hester and Pearl in the daylight?

Chapter 13 – Another View of Hester

Review Questions

  1. What was the "terrible machinery" operating on Dimmesdale's wellbeing?

  2. Why did Hester gain the regard of the townspeople?

  3. How did some of them reinterpret Hester's "A"?

  4. What was Hester's error? How did she resolve to fix it?

Thought Questions

  1. Does human nature love more readily than it hates?

  2. What is "woman's strength"? How is it different from man's strength?

  3. What makes thoughts dangerous?

  4. Hawthorne said of Hester, "The scarlet letter had not done its office." Explain.

Chapter 14 – Hester and the Physician

Review Questions

  1. Why didn't Hester want the scarlet letter removed?

  2. How had Chillingworth changed?

  3. What caused the transformation?

  4. What did Hester plan to do?

Thought Questions

  1. Was Chillingworth's downfall Hester's fault? Whose was it?

  2. What did Chillingworth mean when he called their paths "fate"?

Chapter 15 – Hester and Pearl

Review Questions
1. What wrong had Chillingworth done to Hester?
2. How much did Pearl understand about Hester's "A"?
3. What did Hester tell Pearl? Why?

Chapter 16 – A Forest Walk

Review Questions
1. Why didn't Hester want to meet Dimmesdale in his study?
2. Where did she meet him?
3. What marked Dimmesdale's suffering?

Thought Questions
1. Were Pearl's questions about the scarlet letter wholly innocent? Discuss.

Chapter 17 – The Pastor and His Parishioner

Review Questions
1. Why did Dimmesdale find relief in meeting Hester?
2. What did Hester reveal to Dimmesdale?
3. What couldn't Hester bear?
4. What advice did Hester give Dimmesdale?

Thought Questions
1. Why did Hawthorne describe Hester and Dimmesdale as ghosts?
2. Would atheism have given Dimmesdale the peace he sought? Why or why not?
3. Can a ruined soul help others toward salvation?
4. Was Chillingworth's sin the worst of the three? Discuss.

Chapter 18 – A Flood of Sunshine

Review Questions
1. What did Hester and Dimmesdale plan to do?
2. What did Hester do to symbolize her resolve?

Chapter 19 – The Child at the Brook-Side

Review Questions
1. Why had Dimmesdale been afraid of Pearl?
2. Why did Pearl refuse to cross the brook?
3. How did Hester convince her to come forward?
4. How did Pearl treat Dimmesdale?

Thought Questions
1. Do children always forge a link between their parents? Why?
2. Is it symbolic that Pearl would not allow Hester to leave off the scarlet letter? If so, how?

Chapter 20 – The Minister in a Maze

Review Questions
1. Where had Hester and Dimmesdale decided to go?
2. Why was Dimmesdale glad for the delayed departure?

   3. What did Mistress Hibbins suggest to Dimmesdale?

Thought Questions
   1. Why did Dimmesdale struggle with the temptation when he returned from the forest?
   2. Had Dimmesdale made a bargain with the devil? In what way?

Chapter 21 – The New England Holiday

Review Questions
   1. Why did Pearl call Dimmesdale a strange man?
   2. What characterized the "incomplete morality of the age"?
   3. What did the ship's commander tell Hester?

Thought Questions
   1. What gives a law its power? Threats of punishment? General agreement?

Chapter 22 – The Procession

Review Questions
   1. Who were the highest ranking members of the procession?
   2. What gave them prestige?
   3. How was Dimmesdale different when he passed Hester and Pearl?
   4. What message did the seaman send Hester through Pearl?

Chapter 23 – The Revelation

Review Questions
   1. How was Dimmesdale's sermon received?
   2. What did Dimmesdale do when he reached the scaffold?
   3. How did Chillingworth react?
   4. What was Dimmesdale's announcement?
   5. What happened to him after he gave it?

Thought Questions
   1. Why was the scaffold the only place Dimmesdale could escape Chillingworth?
   2. Why did Pearl suddenly accept Dimmesdale?
   3. How did his acceptance change her?
   4. Is agony a necessary part of redemption? Discuss.

Chapter 24 – Conclusion

Review Questions
   1. What had been on Dimmesdale's heart?
   2. How did some witnesses explain away his guilt?
   3. What was the overarching moral of *The Scarlet Letter*?
   4. How did Chillingworth change after Dimmesdale died? Why?
   5. To whom did Chillingworth leave his property?
   6. What happened to Hester and Pearl?
   7. What was the motto of Hester's story?

Thought Questions
1. Which explanation of the mark on Dimmesdale's chest do you agree with? Why?
2. Is it always best to display your worst to the world? What does it mean to "be true"?
3. Are hate and love essentially the same thing?
4. Is this a story of redemption? Why or why not?

Hand Work
PROOFREADING

For this practice session, you will need to work on proofreading for organization and transitions. Below are five topic sentences for an essay on *The Scarlet Letter*. Assume that each sentence represents a paragraph in the essay. One topic sentence represents the introduction, and one represents the conclusion. Look at the sentences and decide whether or not to change the order in which they appear. Make sure the flow of the paper is logical when you are finished: there is not one "right" answer, but you should be able to give a reason for organizing the essay in a particular way.

Thesis: In *The Scarlet Letter*, Pearl represents the act of sin and demonstrates how difficult it is to hide.

A. Pearl's actions help Chillingworth uncover Dimmesdale's sin.

B. Humans attempt to hide and contain sin, but sin usually becomes visible despite our efforts.

C. Dimmesdale feels responsible for Pearl, and Pearl claims ownership of him as well.

D. Hawthorne uses Pearl as a deeper symbol of sin and its uncontrollable effects.

E. Hester treats Pearl as a "living scarlet letter" and cannot control her actions.

After you have put the topic sentences in order, your next task is to write a one- or two-sentence transition between the "paragraphs" of this essay. Look at the example, and do the same for the topic sentences you have just rearranged.

Example

Thesis: *The Scarlet Letter* suggests that sin can have physical as well as spiritual effects.

A. Chillingworth's physical changes mirror the change of "righteous anger" to desire for vengeance.

B. Dimmesdale's physical illness is a result of his attempts to hide his sin.

Transition: Chillingworth is physically affected by sin when he begins to act with evil intent. On the other hand, Dimmesdale shows the physical effects of sin when he tries to cover up existing sin.

The Red Badge of Courage
Stephen Crane

Stephen Crane (1871-1900) had a short, but successful career as a writer. Crane was born in New Jersey, where as a young man he began to write stories about the communities in which he lived. By the time he was twenty-one, he had already written his first novel as well as multiple stories and news articles. Later, as a young man he traveled extensively while covering the events of the Spanish American War and the Greco-Turkish War. As a war correspondent, Crane saw a brutal side of humanity that figured prominently into his writing. *The Red Badge of Courage*, set during the Civil War, is a good example of Crane's naturalistic, stark pictures of human interactions. The novel was published in 1895, just five years before Crane died at the age of twenty-eight.

Chapter 1

Review Questions
1. What did the tall soldier report?
2. Why had Henry been disappointed by his mother's farewell?
3. What surprised Henry about military life?
4. Why couldn't Henry trust the veterans?
5. What was Henry afraid would happen in the first battle? What reassured him?

Thought Questions
1. Has "throat-grappling" warfare disappeared? If so, is it because men are better or because they are more timid? Explain.
2. Does pride give you strength? In what way?
3. Is it possible to know war without experiencing it?

Chapter 2

Review Questions
1. Did the regiment go into battle the following morning?
2. What did the fat soldier attempt to steal? Did the regiment support him?

3. Did Wilson think he would run? Why or why not?

Thought Questions
1. What do you think influences whether or not a soldier runs from battle?

Chapter 3

Review Questions
1. What separated the infantries of theory and practice?
2. How could passers still tell Henry's regiment was new?
3. Why did Henry think the regiment was trapped?
4. What was Henry and the loud soldier's biggest complaint?
5. How did Henry view death?
6. What did the loud soldier give Henry? Why?

Thought Questions
1. Why did Henry say he had not voluntarily enlisted?
2. Henry hoped to find the answer to what Question in the dead man?
3. Does a man become another thing in battle? Explain.

Chapter 4

Review Questions
1. Describe the battle.
2. Did Henry see the enemy?

Chapter 5

Review Questions
1. What did the general ask the colonel to do?
2. How did Henry change after he fired his first shot?
3. Did Henry's regiment succeed in their task?

Chapter 6

Review Questions
1. Was the battle over?
2. What began to happen to the regiment?
3. What did Henry do?
4. What did Henry overhear the general say?

Thought Questions
1. Crane compares soldiers to "slaves toiling in the temple of this god." What god? Discuss.
2. "Death about to thrust him between the shoulder blades was far more dreadful than death about to smite him between the eyes." Why?

Chapter 7

Review Questions
1. How did Henry justify his actions to himself?
2. What did Henry take as a sign he had done the right thing?
3. What frightened him in the woods?

Chapter 8

Review Questions
1. Which way did Henry run? Why?
2. What did the tattered soldier tell Henry? What did he ask him?

Chapter 9

Review Questions
1. Who was the spectral soldier? What happened to him?
2. What was strange about the way Jim died?

Chapter 10

Review Questions
1. Why "couldn't" the tattered man die?
2. Why did Henry leave him?
3. What was Henry's crime?

Chapter 11

Review Questions
1. Why did the retreating wagons comfort Henry?
2. What effect did the forward-going infantry have on Henry? What kept him from joining them?
3. Why did Henry stay near the battle?

Thought Questions
1. Did Henry want his army to win the battle? Explain.
2. Why do individuals need the kind of moral vindication Henry talked about?
3. What did Henry mean when he expressed fear of becoming "a slang phrase"?

Chapter 12

Review Questions
1. How was Henry injured?
2. What did the stranger help Henry do?

Chapter 13

Review Questions
1. What did Henry tell Wilson?
2. What did Wilson do for Henry?

Chapter 14

Review Questions
1. What was the "soldier's bath"?
2. How had Wilson changed since the camp days?
3. Who did Wilson think was winning the battle? Who did Henry think?
4. What had happened to half of the regiment on the first day in battle?

Thought Questions
1. Does war change people for good or for bad? On what does the answer depend?
2. Henry "climbed a peak of wisdom from which he could perceive himself as a very wee thing." Explain.

Chapter 15

Review Questions
1. What did Henry remember? Why didn't he tell Wilson?
2. What lesson had Henry learned from the first day?
3. How did Henry mentally separate himself from the other men who had run?
4. What did Wilson ask Henry to give him?

Thought Questions
1. "He had performed his mistakes in the dark, so he [Henry] was still a man." Do your misdeeds only matter if they are seen by others? Why or why not?
2. Once Henry became "comfortable and contented," he no longer wanted to "set things straight." Have you ever shared this feeling?

Chapter 16

Review Questions
1. To what job was Henry's regiment assigned?
2. Whom did Henry blame for the loss?
3. What caused Henry to stop bragging?
4. Why did the Lieutenant scold Henry?

Thought Questions
1. Are rumors more or less powerful during times of war? Why?

Chapter 17

Review Questions
1. Why did Henry begin to hate the opposing army?
2. Why did one of Henry's comrades tell him to stop shooting?

Thought Questions
1. If you think you are going to fail, do you work harder? Why or why not?
2. Are heroes usually aware of the process of becoming a hero? Explain.

Chapter 18

Review Questions
1. Who had been shot during the first attack?
2. What news did Henry and Wilson overhear?
3. What did Henry learn from the exchange?
4. What was Henry and Wilson's "ironical secret"?

Chapter 19

Review Questions
1. What happened when the men slowed their charge?
2. Who got the regiment to move again the second time it paused?
3. What love awoke in Henry as he ran?
4. What did Henry and Wilson rescue?

Thought Questions
1. The charge had "a temporary but sublime absence of selfishness." What prompted that feeling?
2. Henry attributed power to the flag because "no harm could come to it." Why?

Chapter 20

Review Questions
1. What did Henry hate most? Why?
2. What did the Lieutenant discover?
3. What effect did the small duel have on the regiment?

Chapter 21

Review Questions
1. Why were the men especially afraid during the last leg of the journey?
2. Why did the commanding officer reproach the regiment?
3. What did the colonel and the lieutenant say about Henry's fighting?

Chapter 22

Review Questions
1. Whom did Henry blame for his suffering? What did he see as the best revenge?

Chapter 23

Review Questions
1. What did the regiment have to do?
2. What did Henry hope to accomplish in the clash?
3. Who took the enemy's flag?

Chapter 24

Review Questions
1. To where was the regiment summoned?
2. How did Henry's mind change as they marched?
3. How did Henry explain his initial flight?
4. What one thing did Henry regret? How did he overcome his regret?

Thought Questions
1. What does it mean to be a man?
2. Is it a good thing to utilize your sins? Explain.
3. What does it mean to be tiny but not inconsequent? Have you ever experienced this feeling?

Brain Work
CONDUCTING (secondary) RESEARCH

If you were writing an essay about the historical accuracy of *The Red Badge of Courage*, what kind of information would you need? Where would you be most likely to find that information? Keep in mind that this book is based on the real Civil War Battle of Chancellorsville.

Your goal is to find five sources that you could potentially use to write an essay of this type. You may use Internet sources, but at least three of your sources should be books.

Go to your local library and find three sources about *The Red Badge of Courage* and/or the Civil War. Try to find at least one book about Stephen Crane. Look at the table of contents in each book to find chapters that would be helpful if you were actually writing this paper.

If you have access to the Internet, go online and carefully search the Battle of Chancellorsville and *The Red Badge of Courage*. Google [www.google.com] is a good all-around search engine. When you are conducting Internet research, use very specific search terms; you will get more targeted (and sometimes more reliable) information.

For each Internet source, remember to check reliability. If the organization sponsoring the site has an "About Us" page, this is a great place to look for source information. Historical sites sponsored by the government, by a private foundation, or by a university may have helpful information. Focus on the organization's credentials and any information available about the researchers who did the work. The date is not as important since you are dealing with a historic subject.

For extra practice, try making a works cited page for your resources, using correct MLA format.

"The Pit and the Pendulum"

Edgar A. Poe

Edgar Allan Poe (1809-1849) was one of the first masters of the short story form, as well as a leading writer of crime and horror fiction. Orphaned as a child, Poe was raised by the Allans of Richmond, Virginia. Already an avid writer, by the time Poe left the University of Virginia, he was preparing to publish his first collection of poems. After serving for two years in the U.S. Army, Poe took a temporary post at West Point, and then left to pursue a full-time writing career. Much of the rest of his life, particularly the mode of his death, remains a mystery. "The Pit and the Pendulum," a typically dark and haunting story, was first published in 1842.

Review Questions
1. What was the speaker's sentence? Who sentenced him?
2. Why did the judges vanish?
3. What are the two stages of awakening from a swoon, according to Poe?
4. Where did the speaker awake?
5. What did he call "the most hideous of fates"?
6. How did he know when he had circled the room?
7. What did he discover when he tried to cross the room?
8. What did the man see when he awoke the second time? What had changed?
9. Why did the painting of Time worry him so much?
10. Why couldn't the pendulum cut his bonds?
11. How did he escape? What happened when he did?
12. What happened to the cell walls?
13. Who caught the man's hand just before he fell?

Thought Questions
1. Poe said, "Even in the grave, all is *not* lost." Explain. Do you agree?
2. Would you prefer "direct physical agonies" or "most hideous moral horrors" in death? Why?
3. "It was *hope* that prompted the nerve to quiver – the frame to shrink." Does hope cause fear?

4. Why was the pit the speaker's greatest fear?

5. The review questions follow standard practice and refer to the speaker as a man. Does Poe ever concretely establish that his character is male? What makes the character seem masculine?

Hand Work
FORMATTING CITATIONS

1. Below is the bibliography information for several fictional sources. For practice, put them in proper MLA format and order (alphabetical by last name) for a works cited page.

Author: Alice Thomas. Title: *Edgar Allen Poe: A Biography*. Publisher: Greenwood Press, New York. Date: 1984.

Authors: Lee Thomas, Edwin Marsh. Title: *Edgar Allen Poe's Telling Heart*. Publisher: Oxford University Press, London. Date: 2000.

Author: Jack Carne. Title: "Symbolism in 'The Pit and the Pendulum.'" Publication: *Literary Analysis*, volume 3, issue 4. Date: May 2003.

Author: Edgar Allen Poe. Title: "The Pit and the Pendulum." In: *The Collected Stories of E.A. Poe*, edited by Lindsay Elwood, pages 114-131. Publisher: HarperCollins, New York. Date: 1997.

2. Read through the paragraph below. You want to use it in your essay, but you don't want to quote it directly. Without looking at it, paraphrase it on a separate sheet of paper, putting it in your own words AND sentence structure.

> When Edgar Allen Poe wrote "The Pit and the Pendulum," he was heavily influenced by the sense of failure that hung over his own life. His unhappy childhood and fractured adulthood allowed him to describe the despair of his main character with overwhelming accuracy.

3. The first paragraph is an essay section that has been paraphrased from the second paragraph. Compare the two and circle parts of the paraphrase that are too close to the original either in wording or in sentence structure. After you finish, decide whether or not you would classify the paragraph as plagiarism. Be prepared to defend your answer.

Paraphrased Paragraph

> Edgar Allen Poe's "The Pit and the Pendulum" is one of his most well-known stories. It deals with mental and physical torture, courage, fear, and finally, salvation. Poe's hero is both the main character of a horror story and the imperfect subject of a psychological study of human nature (Windham 12).

Original Paragraph (fictional)

> "The Pit and the Pendulum" is one of Edgar Allen Poe's most famous short stories. Set during the Spanish Inquisition, "The Pit and the Pendulum" discusses themes of mental and physical torture, fear, courage, and ultimately,

salvation. Poe's nameless protagonist is both the downtrodden hero of a horror story and the flawed subject of a psychological quest to understand human nature.

Through Gates of Splendor
Elisabeth Elliot

Elisabeth Elliot (1926–2015) was born in Belgium into a family of missionaries. After college, where she studied languages, Elliot traveled to Ecuador to live among the Quichua Indians. While in Ecuador, she married Jim Elliot and served with him until he was killed with four other missionaries while trying to connect with the previously unreached Auca (Huaorani) Indians. After her husband's death, Elliot stayed in Ecuador and continued to minister to the Aucas for two years, then returned to work among the Quichua until she returned to the United States in 1963. *Through Gates of Splendor*, Elliot's account of the events leading up to and following the missionaries' deaths, was published in 1957.

Chapter 1 – "I Dare Not Stay Home"

Review Questions
1. Where was Jim going? Why?
2. Which tribe had resisted all approaches by the white man?
3. What effect had rubber trade had on the country?
4. Where did Jim and Elisabeth meet?
5. Who became Jim's traveling companion?

Thought Questions
1. Can Christian love "wipe out the memories of past treachery and brutality"?
2. What do you lose in translating something from the original language?
3. Do you agree with Jim that there is no value in attainment? Discuss.
4. Jim spoke of "joking with God." Do you think God has a sense of humor?

Chapter 2 – Destination: Shandia

Review Questions
1. Why did Jim and Pete have to stay in Quito?
2. Why did they call Ecuador the "land of mañana"?
3. Why had Dr. Tidmarsh left Shandia?

Chapter 3 – "All Things to All Men"

Review Questions
1. What did the Quichua boys find odd about Jim and Pete?
2. Why was the machete so important in Quichua life?
3. What did "dying" mean to the Quichua?

Thought Questions
1. Why is it important to know the language of the people to whom you minister?
2. Why did the Indians themselves need to be the answer?

Chapter 4 – Infinite Adaptability

Review Questions
1. Who joined Jim and Pete in Shandia?
2. Why did Ed leave law school?
3. Why did Jim and Pete send word for Ed to come immediately to Shandia?

Thought Questions
1. Is it "putting all your eggs in one basket" to trust God? Is it a risk?
2. Are people who have not committed a crime fundamentally different from those who have?
3. Ed and Marilou both wanted to "be an influence upon the other for closer fellowship with the Lord." What would that look like in a relationship?

Chapter 5 – "Expendable for God"

Review Questions
1. Who was Nate Saint?
2. What was the purpose of the MAF?
3. What had prevented Nate from flying for the Air Force?

Thought Questions
1. What kinds of things become "unnecessary cargo" that weighs you down?
2. Why did Elliot recount Nate's engineering feats? How did they relate to his missionary work?
3. Are safety precautions evidence of a lack of trust? Discuss.

Chapter 6 – Missionary to the Head-Shrinking Jivaros

Review Questions
1. What ended Roger Youderian's hopes of a musical career?
2. What did missionaries have to accomplish before they could make contact with primitive tribes?

Thought Questions
1. Describe the Jivaro culture. Is our culture similar in any way? If so, how?
2. Do you think missionaries struggle with pride? Explain.

Chapter 7 – Breaking Jungle Barriers

Review Questions
1. Why did Roger move to Wambimi? How did he gain a meeting with the Atshuara chief?

2. Why was Roger in such a hurry when the Nate landed on the new airstrip?

Thought Questions
  1. Is physical care or spiritual care the most important part of missionary work? Why?

Chapter 8 – The Aucas

Review Questions
  1. Why did the Aucas hate white people?
  2. Why did Don Carlos know so much about the Aucas?
  3. Who was Dayuma? What did she tell the missionaries about the Aucas?

Thought Questions
  1. Were the Aucas justified for hating white people? Is hate ever justified?
  2. When does a situation become "too late" for peace?

Chapter 9 – September, 1955

Review Questions
  1. Why was Arajuno a strategic outpost?
  2. Who were the five families who would reach out to the Aucas?

Thought Questions
  1. "I will die in your words." How is this different from other prayers of faith? How is it the same?
  2. Should missionaries who are engaged in dangerous work stay single? Support your answer.
  3. Is it hypocritical for a missionary to have an electric fence and burglar alarm? Why or why not?

Chapter 10 – Operation Auca Begins

Review Questions
  1. Why did the missionaries keep their approaches to the Aucas a secret?
  2. What problems stood in their way?

Chapter 11 – A Line from Plane to Ground

Review Questions
  1. Why was the spiraling-line technique so important?
  2. What gifts did the missionaries give the Aucas?

Thought Questions
  1. Why did the missionaries give the Aucas trinkets and ribbons? Were they judging unfairly?
  2. Nate called Aucas "stone age people." Was this accurate or a stereotype? What is the difference?

Chapter 12 – The Savages Respond

Review Questions
  1. Who was the most conservative about landing among the Aucas? The most impatient?

  2. What did the Aucas give the missionaries in return?
  3. What personal struggle did Roger face? How was it resolved?

Thought Questions
  1. Were the Aucas more "savage" than other humans?
  2. Nate recorded, "We didn't feel that [the old man] warranted too good a gift." Were the missionaries manipulative in their gift-giving? Discuss.
  3. If God calls missionaries to a certain role, does he allow them to fail? Why or why not?

Chapter 13 – The Search for "Palm Beach"

Review Questions
  1. What surprise did the missionaries see on the roof of No. 3?
  2. What did the missionaries need to do before the first ground meeting?
  3. What did the Quichua do when they learned about the missions to the Aucas?
  4. Why did the missionaries drop pictures of their team members?

Thought Questions
  1. Was it unfair for the missionaries to give the Aucas so many gifts, and not the Quichua?
  2. How would you describe the relationship between the missionaries and the Auca Indians?

Chapter 14 – An Auca on the Path

Review Questions
  1. What made the missionaries hurry to make contact on the ground?
  2. Why had the Aucas come to Arajuno?

Chapter 15 – Why Did the Men Go?

Review Questions
  1. How did the Aucas feel about the missionaries? How did the missionaries know?
  2. What was the "condition of true discipleship" in marriage?
  3. Why were the men driven to go to the Aucas?

Thought Questions
  1. "He is no fool who gives what he cannot keep to gain what he cannot lose." Discuss.
  2. If missionaries die without leading their community to Christ, have they failed?
  3. The men carried weapons so "the white man held the upper hand." Was this the right attitude?

Chapter 16 – "We Go Not Forth Alone"

Review Questions
  1. Why did Nate feel a particular weight the night before the mission?
  2. What made the landing and takeoff at Palm Beach so difficult?
  3. How did the men know their beach camp was being watched?
  4. What worried Nate about the missionaries' growing "friendly feeling" toward the Aucas?

Chapter 17 – Success on Friday

Review Questions
1. Who were the first Aucas to respond to the men's invitations?
2. Where did Nate take "George" in the plane?
3. When did the Aucas leave? Did they return the next day?

Thought Questions
1. What do you think the Aucas were saying to one another when they met the missionaries?

Chapter 18 – Silence

Review Questions
1. What happened at the arranged time for radio contact?
2. What did Johnny find on the beach?
3. What had happened to the missionaries?
4. What made the return of the rescue party doubly difficult?

Thought Questions
1. What is the best way to tell someone bad news?
2. How does self-pity "rot away a life"?

Chapter 19 – "Yet Have We Not Forgotten Thee"

Review Questions
1. What conclusions did the widows draw about their husbands' final hours?
2. Whose lives were changed by these events?
3. How did the widows plan to continue their husbands' work?

Thought Questions
1. Why do you think the Aucas turned against the missionaries?
2. Was the price too great? Did the men waste their lives?

Epilogue (November 1958)

Review Questions
1. Where did Elisabeth Elliot go in 1958?
2. How had the Aucas made contact with Elliot?
3. Why had the Aucas killed the missionaries?

Thought Questions
1. What kind of strength would it take to sit as friends with someone who killed your spouse? How do you get that kind of strength?

Epilogue II (January 1981)

Review Questions
1. What happened to the widows?
2. To what did the Aucas' name change? Why did it change?
3. How should you understand the story of *Through Gates of Splendor*?

Thought Questions
1. How are spiritual and physical fitness similar? How are they different?

2. Why do you think Elliot mentioned the weaknesses and flaws of the continuing mission to the Waorani? Did she blot her husband's work by doing so? Explain.

3. What effect, if any, does a story like Elisabeth Elliot's have on you? Explain.

Brain Work
CONSIDERING FORM AND STYLE

Writing professionally is a valuable skill to learn, and will greatly improve your essays. In addition, it is an important skill to practice in case you ever need to address sensitive or controversial topics in a respectful manner.

In the following paragraph, find and highlight or circle as many errors in professionalism as you can find. Common examples are using first or second person pronouns (I, me, we, you), contractions (don't, can't, won't), and slang or improper grammar. Then rewrite the paragraph, giving it a professional tone.

NOTE: When you are picking out contractions, remember to differentiate between apostrophes used to indicate possession and apostrophes used in contractions. Possessive apostrophes should not be changed.

Elisabeth Elliot's book *Through Gates of Splendor* made me ask interesting questions about what it means to be a missionary. While Elliot tells you about the courage of her husband, Jim Elliot, and the other missionaries to the Auca Indians, she doesn't try to make them out to be saints (not even Nate). The flaws and human struggles of the missionaries are what made me like them. For example, Roger Youderian got depressed and felt defeated. As a result, he almost left Ecuador, planning to drop out of missionary activities altogether. In the end, he didn't give up; he stuck around to help the others. The other missionaries' problems aren't mentioned as directly, but their diaries and letters show people who felt pride, fear, recklessness, and indecision, and who even got down in the dumps sometimes. Since these men and their wives were messed up humans like me and you, it's doubly inspiring to see the way God used their love of him to reach the Waorani Indians of Ecuador.

Born Again
Charles Colson

harles Colson (1931–2012) grew up in Boston, and after college, he attended law school, all the while volunteering for various political campaigns. Colson eventually ended up in Washington, where he served from 1969 to 1973 as Special Counsel to President Nixon. A notoriously hard-hitting politician, Colson was indicted in 1974 for events concerning the 1972 break-in at the Democratic National Committee's headquarters in the Watergate office complex. Before his indictment, Colson had converted to evangelical Christianity, and after he was released from prison in 1975, he founded Prison Fellowship, a Christian organization providing community and outreach to prison inmates. His autobiography, *Born Again*, was first published in 1976.

Chapter 1 – Something Wrong

Review Questions
1. Why was election night not the proudest of Colson's life?
2. Why did President Nixon want to see Colson?
3. What did Colson describe as the "paradox of Richard Nixon"?
4. Why did the president convene his staff early the next morning?

Thought Questions
1. Colson portrayed Nixon as demonstrating "rare courage" but also "unable to show charity." How do these two images fit together?
2. Is it always wise to accept someone for what they are in their "best moments"?

Chapter 2 – "Good Enough"

Review Questions
1. What one word summed up what was important to Colson?
2. Describe Colson's early family life and education.
3. What prevented Colson from attending Harvard?
4. Why was Colson's Marine battalion sent to Guatemala?
5. How did Colson secure Saltonstall's 1960 Senate bid?

Thought Questions
1. What does it mean to be "good enough"?
2. Are ethics different in politics? Should they be?
3. Why do you think the adoption agency turned down Colson and his wife? Do you think they made the right decision?
4. Discuss Colson's expectation that working with the president would give him fulfillment.

Chapter 3 – "Break All the __ China"

Review Questions
1. How did Colson offend Attorney General John Mitchell?
2. What did Colson do to obtain the commission on Catholic schools?
3. What happened at Kent State University on May 4, 1970?
4. Why did Nixon choose to invade Cambodia?
5. What did the idea of "linkage" have to do with Nixon's new design for foreign policy?

Thought Questions
1. What was Colson's early *modus operandi* as a politician? Is it possible to separate a political identity from a personal identity?
2. Who was responsible for the violence at the protests?
3. Can politicians afford to be personal? Is it possible to balance the big picture and the concerns of individuals?
4. From where do presidents derive their power?
5. What should be the proper relationship between the press and politicians?

Chapter 4 – The President's Night Out

Review Questions
1. What did Colson mean by the "era of the 'Imperial' presidency"? How did the Kennedy Center incident exemplify that mindset?

Thought Questions
1. Why do you think Colson included the incident with the Kennedy Center? What does it reveal about Nixon? About Colson?

Chapter 5 – Hatchet Man

Review Questions
1. How did Colson earn the name "Hatchet Man"?
2. What major leak to the press began in June 1971? Who was responsible?
3. How did Nixon's people retaliate? Who were "the Plumbers"?
4. What proved to be the deathblow to Muskie's campaign?
5. What effect did Nixon's decision to mine the Haiphang Harbor have on the 1972 election?
6. What happened in June 1972? How was the incident linked to Nixon's administration?

Thought Questions
1. What do you think is the proper limit on the free flow of information?
2. What is the difference between recognizing an act as stupid and as morally wrong?

3. Explain Colson's claim, "We had set in motion forces that would sooner or later make Watergate, or something like it, inevitable." What forces did he mean?

Chapter 6 – "Exhausted Volcano"

Review Questions
1. What changed during Nixon's second term?
2. What happened to the Vietnam peace treaty shortly after the election?
3. What caused the split between Nixon and Kissinger?
4. What was Colson's last official act as Special Counsel?
5. What had changed in the tone at the White House when he returned?

Thought Questions
1. What do you think was bothering Colson after the re-election?
2. Colson suggested that to be in politics for too long was unhealthy. Do you think this is true of all careers, or is there something especially taxing about politics?
3. Colson portrayed Nixon as what kind of man? If you have read other accounts of the Nixon presidency, how do they compare?

Chapter 7 – The Long Hot Summer

Review Questions
1. What was Colson's association with the Raytheon Company?
2. How had Tom Phillips changed?
3. Why was Colson's role in Watergate considered an "obstruction of justice"?
4. What was the Ervin Committee?
5. Who were Bob Woodward and Carl Bernstein?
6. What were the results of Colson's polygraph test about Watergate?
7. What conclusion did prosecutor Earl Silbert draw about Colson?

Thought Questions
1. What does it mean to have a full life?
2. "It is almost impossible to counteract an untruthful press report that circulates the nation—like trying to retrieve the feathers shaken loose from a pillow in a high wind." Why? Is telling the truth always enough to counteract a rumor?
3. Did it matter to Colson's job if Nixon were lying? Should it have mattered?
4. Why do you think Watergate created such an "overwhelming madness"?

Chapter 8 – An Unforgettable Night

Review Questions
1. What had led to Tom Phillips's conversion? How did Colson respond to the story?
2. What book did Phillips suggest that Colson read?
3. What is "foxhole religion"?

Thought Questions
1. Phillips said, "You had to destroy [your enemies] because you couldn't trust in yourselves." Explain. Is it that simple?
2. Is it possible to survive in politics without a dog-eat-dog mindset? Discuss.
3. Why do you think pride is such a difficult vice to admit? Do you agree with Lewis?

Chapter 9 – Cottage by the Sea

Review Questions
1. Where did Colson like to go when he needed rejuvenation?
2. What was the difference between law and moral law, according to Lewis/Colson?
3. What questions did Colson feel he needed to answer about God?
4. How did Colson's view of the individual begin to change as a result of his study?

Thought Questions
1. Describe Colson's process of analyzing Christianity. Do his arguments make sense to you? What additional questions would you add to his list?
2. How did Lewis/Colson sum up the essence of Christianity?
3. Is the individual more or less important than the stage? What is the basis of your answer?

Chapter 10 – Washington Revisited

Review Questions
1. How did Colson's outlook change after his conversion?
2. What did Colson discover about the presence of other Christians in Washington?
3. What was the result of Colson's hearing before the grand jury?
4. Why was Colson unwilling to plead the fifth before the Ervin Committee? Why did he have to do it?

Thought Questions
1. Should some beliefs be able to transcend politics? If so, which ones?
2. What role did race play in Colson's hearing? Do you think Colson's representation is a fair one? Discuss.
3. Colson said, "There is no joy among politicians in witnessing one of their own, even a bitter foe, not just defeated but helpless, shamed, the last vestige of self-respect stripped from him." Why might this be so?

Chapter 11 – Brothers

Review Questions
1. Who was Harold Hughes?
2. How was the meeting with Hughes different from other political gatherings Colson had attended?
3. What happened to Vice President Agnew?
4. What was the purpose of Fellowship House?

Thought Questions
1. What does fellowship mean? Is it important to have common interests? What shared characteristics are the most and least important?

Chapter 12 – Christ in the Headlines

Review Questions
1. What surprise visitor showed up to sit next to Colson at the prayer breakfast?
2. Why didn't Colson want to broadcast his faith to the press?
3. How did Colson respond to the media attention?
4. What did the prosecutors expect would follow Colson's conversion?
5. What letter changed Colson's perspective on the situation?

Thought Questions
1. Did Colson need to apologize to Burns? Why or why not?
2. How is the word *conversion* understood today? How would you define it?
3. Discuss the backlash that came in response to Colson's conversion. Do you think the cynicism was justified?

Chapter 13 – The Lonely House

Review Questions
1. Why did Nixon want to see Colson after the CBS broadcast?
2. What was Colson's response when Nixon asked about his conversion?
3. What concern led Nixon to call Colson again that night?

Thought Questions
1. Why do you think Colson was twice unable to tell Nixon about his new faith?
2. Are self-interest and high patriotic motive closely related? How do you tell them apart?
3. How did Colson's relationship to Nixon change after his conversion? Why?

Chapter 14 – Underground Movement

Review Questions
1. Who was the new special prosecutor after Cox?
2. How did Arthur and Helen Burns respond to Colson's confession?
3. What did reporter Nick Thimmesch call an "underground movement"?
4. Who was the first political figure indicted for Watergate?
5. Why were the government officials particularly afraid of going to prison?

Thought Questions
1. What is the role of humor in dealing with unpleasant events? When is it appropriate or inappropriate?
2. Why do you think it was harder for Colson to talk to his family than to strangers about his conversion?

Chapter 15 – Accused

Review Questions
1. What did Colson believe the prosecution was asking from him?
2. Why was Colson unable, ethically, to agree to the plea bargain?
3. What had been the CIA's role in Watergate?
4. How many and which people were finally indicted in the Watergate cover-up?

Thought Questions
1. "How can anyone ever be sure he isn't even subconsciously tempted to offer up testimony more to the prosecutor's liking than the facts really warrant? When a good deal is hanging in the balance, is it not human nature to do so?" How would you answer these questions?
2. Was it fair for Colson's wife and children to be scarred by his mistakes? Was it avoidable?

Chapter 16 – Decision

Review Questions
1. How did the other members of the fellowship respond when Colson volunteered to drop out?
2. What was the defense's strategy for seeking a delay in one of Colson's cases? What was the result?
3. What did the taped White House conversations reveal?
4. What dilemma did Colson face as the impeachment hearings began?
5. Describe the interview with Mike Wallace for CBS.
6. What did Colson's father most want to know about the trials when Colson visited him in the hospital?
7. What did Colson resolve to do, and why?

Thought Questions
1. Why did Colson think the failed effort to gain a delay had been "worth it all"? Do you agree?
2. Do presidents have the right to a "private side"? Discuss.
3. "A new Christian, besides talking to his God, does he do no penance for deeds like that?" What do you think?
4. Colson said, "Legal niceties make moral nonsense." Do you agree?
5. What is the difference between a government of law and a government of men?

Chapter 17 – Guilty, Your Honor

Review Questions
1. Did Judge Gesell and the prosecutors agree to Colson's plea?
2. How did Gordon Liddy respond when Colson entered the courtroom? Why?
3. What did Colson describe as the ramifications of being a felon?

Chapter 18 – Awaiting Judgment

Review Questions
1. What did the press and opposition assume Colson's guilty plea would mean?
2. Why did the Judicial Committee strike Colson from its witness list?
3. What advice about prison did Colson receive from Bud Krogh?

Thought Questions
1. What was the effect of Colson's sentencing on his children? Why do innocent people suffer from others' moral choices?
2. Discuss Bud Krogh's advice to Colson. Was it sound advice? Was it problematic in any way?

Chapter 19 – The Fall of the Gavel

Review Questions
1. Why did Judge Gesell interrupt Shapiro's final plea on Colson's behalf?
2. What was Colson's sentence?

Thought Questions
1. Was Colson's sentence fair? How did Colson, in writing this book, portray the court proceedings?
2. Do you agree with Gesell that "morality is a higher force than expediency"?

Chapter 20 – The Slammer

Review Questions

1. Where was Colson initially incarcerated?
2. When did Nixon finally resign?
3. What had Nixon's aides hoped he would do for them before he left the presidency?
4. What other Watergate figure joined Colson at Holabird?
5. What news from his family did Colson receive while in prison? What did he find out about his father as a result?

Thought Questions

1. What is your impression of prison conditions? On what is your idea based?
2. Do you agree that "it is the hearts of men that for better or worse change the course of human history, not the man-made organs of government"?
3. Discuss the policy of granting pardons. Do you think it is a just practice? Should presidents have that power? Why or why not?

Chapter 21 – "Don't Get Involved"

Review Questions

1. To what prison was Colson transferred?
2. What was the "formula for survival" in prison?
3. Why was Colson careful to receive no favors from the warden?

Thought Questions

1. Why do prisons de-individualize prisoners? What is the purpose?
2. How does Colson describe prison life? What do his descriptions tell you about his character?

Chapter 22 – No Favors, Please

Review Questions

1. What information did Jerry, the messman, pass on to Colson?
2. Why was prison life like the military, according to Colson?
3. What job was Colson assigned to do?
4. To what ministry did he feel he would be called after he left prison?

Thought Questions

1. Given the dilemma of family visits to prisoners, would you prefer the roller coaster of seeing family once a week, or the isolation of not seeing them at all? Why?
2. Is it necessary to experience suffering in order to understand it?

Chapter 23 – When Two or More Gather

Review Questions

1. What did the parole hearings mean for Colson and the other prisoners?
2. What happened when Colson broke up the fight in the dorm?
3. How did Colson avoid the trap of the "sleepers"?

Thought Questions

1. Think about Colson's instinct to prevent bloodshed, and then his instinct to lie. What does this suggest to you about his character? About human nature? About fear?

2. What do you think are the greatest flaws of the criminal justice system? Discuss.
3. If someone knows right and wrong but not legal codes, is he or she morally superior to someone who knows legal codes but not the difference between right and wrong? How does the legal system respond to that question?

Chapter 24 – A Helping Hand

Review Questions
1. Who was Lee Corbin? How did he respond to Colson's message?
2. What steps did Colson and the others take to establish a Christian community at Maxwell?
3. How did Colson begin to help his fellow prisoners with their legal affairs?
4. Why, when his friends were visiting, did Colson rant about Jim Howard's case? What was the result?
5. Why were prisoners' wives banned from the weekday church services?

Thought Questions
1. Why would lawyers and doctors not be permitted to practice their professions in prison?
2. Was Colson justified in defying authority by helping his fellow inmates with legal tasks?
3. "Some of the guards seemed more imprisoned than the inmates themselves." Explain.

Chapter 25 – Unexpected Gift

Review Questions
1. What made the winter especially difficult for the prisoners?
2. What happened to Woodie because of the dye smuggling business?
3. Who had been responsible for the threat on Colson's life? How did he find out?

Thought Questions
1. Was Colson's decision to bring in contraband dye wrong if it resulted in a good thing (providing warmth)? Is it justifiable to break "silly" rules?
2. Why do you think Colson described the philosophy of "the end justifies the means" as a trap?
3. Are there other ways to accomplish good besides "slipping into gray morality"? What are some examples?

Chapter 26 – Spiritual Warfare

Review Questions
1. What incidents did Colson attribute to spiritual attack?
2. What was the Prisoner Coordination system? Why did Colson describe it as one of the "harshest forms of punishment"?
3. How did Colson and the other Christians combat the spiritual attacks they faced?
4. What was the result when the men prayed for Cecil Barnes's healing?

Thought Questions
1. Do you think there is a distinction between good and evil men? If so, what is it?
2. Explain, "It is one thing to know the truth in abstract terms; it's something else again to trust, to be bold about it." To what other situations might this statement apply?

Chapter 27 – A Time to be Free

Review Questions
1. Why was Colson transferred back to Holabird prison?
2. What was the result of the sentence reduction motions filed by the four Watergate prisoners?
3. What happened to Colson's son Christian in January 1975?
4. What did Al Quie offer to do for Colson?
5. Why was Colson finally released?

Thought Questions
1. Why is it so hard to be loyal only to the truth? Are other loyalties more natural?
2. Why was Colson disbarred from practicing law? Should former criminals be disbarred?
3. What kind of freedom became more important to Colson than his physical freedom?

Epilogue

Review Questions
1. To what ministry did Colson feel called after his release?
2. Describe the programs Colson established.
3. What is "Angel Tree"?
4. To what cause did Colson ascribe crime? How did he propose to solve it?

Thought Questions
1. How would you describe the contemporary mindset about prisoners and the way they should be treated? Do you agree?
2. Do you think the crisis of this age is still "the abandonment of truth" and "decline of moral values"? Why or why not?
3. What do you think is the cause of crime? What solutions would you propose?

Brain Work
THINKING ABOUT FORM AND STYLE

Although an essay is largely about your thoughts and interpretation, it should still be professionally written. That means writing in third person when possible (not using I, me, you, or we) and using formal language and style (no contractions, slang terms, or colloquialisms).

In a critical essay, it may be difficult to avoid inserting judgments about the characters and plot of the book. It is acceptable to use firm words and make decisive statements about a book. In fact, an essay that is too hesitant and qualifies every statement with "maybe" or "one might think" is as bad as an essay that is too forceful.

Look at the following list of words and phrases. Pick out the words you would classify as informal, unprofessional, or overly harsh. Next, identify the phrases that are overly hesitant. There is not one set of right answers, so make sure you can explain the reason for each designation. The next time you write, try to do the same thing as you read over your own writing.

…one might suggest…

…the consequences imply…

…the decision was stupid…

…what a ridiculous question!

…the author provides insufficient evidence…

…the author obviously didn't think…

…calls into question the truthfulness…

…what was he thinking?

…by disregarding the facts…

…it is possible…

…perhaps what he means is…

…it can be inferred…

…the plot was disorganized…

…the book is poorly written…

…the characters do not change…

…everyone knows…

… you could argue…

…his conclusion was illogical…

Starship Troopers
Robert Heinlein

Robert Heinlein (1907-1988) was born in Missouri and grew up in Kansas City, where he developed a fascination for astronomy and a love of science fiction. He attended the United States Naval Academy and went on to serve in the U.S. Navy, but was forced to retire by chronic seasickness. After a failed attempt to enter politics, Heinlein turned to writing science fiction as an alternative career, publishing his first story in 1939. When World War II began, he returned to work as a civilian engineer for the Navy, but after the war, he continued to write, publishing an extensive list of children's and adult novels and short stories. *Starship Troopers*, a good example of Heinlein's fusion of science fiction and social commentary, was published in 1959, and won the Hugo Award in 1960.

Chapter 1

Review Questions
1. Who is the speaker? What is his name?
2. What was the goal of the raid?
3. Why did Johnnie almost miss the retrieval boat?

Thought Questions
1. Why didn't the sergeant want any heroes in the outfit?
2. Does it make more sense for a chaplain to fight or not to fight?

Chapter 2

Review Questions
1. Why did Johnnie join the Federal Service?
2. Who opposed his decision? What finally convinced him to join?
3. To what role was Johnnie assigned?

Thought Questions
1. Does violence settle anything? How would you define "settle"?
2. "What is the moral difference, if any, between the soldier and the civilian?"

Chapter 3

Review Questions
1. What was Sergeant Zim's cure for the cold?
2. Why did Johnnie call Breckinridge "outclassed" in his fight against Zim?
3. What didn't Jenkins know about sergeants?

Chapter 4

Review Questions
1. Why was boot camp so harsh?
2. How did Johnnie's section keep warm on the overnight march?
3. What happened to Breckinridge?

Chapter 5

Review Questions
1. Why did the instructors occasionally use real bullets in the simulations?
2. What was Hendrick's offense?
3. What information made it more serious? What was his sentence?

Thought Questions
1. What is the purpose of war, in your opinion?
2. Is it ever a soldier's duty to ask questions? If so, when?

Chapter 6

Review Questions
1. How had the trial backfired on Zim and Frankel?
2. What orders did Frankel give Zim?
3. Who sent Johnnie a letter? Why did the letter impress Sergeant Zim?

Thought Questions
1. Does military service give an individual a stronger sense of citizenship?
2. Will military service ever be a prerequisite for citizenship? Would it be a good thing if it did?
3. To Father, citizenship was a "vain and useless thing." What makes citizenship valuable?

Chapter 7

Review Questions
1. Why was Johnnie's service called the "mobile infantry"? What was powered armor?
2. What was Johnnie's mistake? What was his punishment? What two things were odd about it?

Chapter 8

Review Questions
1. In what way was a flogging complementary?
2. Who received capital punishment? For what crime?
3. Why did Mr. Dubois call "juvenile delinquent" a contradiction in terms?

Thought Questions
1. What are the arguments for and against corporal punishment? What do you think?
2. Does man have a moral instinct? If so, where does it come from?
3. Dubois called moral sense, "an elaboration of the instinct to survive." What do you think?
4. Does man have any natural rights?

Chapter 9

Review Questions
1. What made the training more intense at Camp Spooky?
2. What happened in Seattle?
3. What percentage of the regiment graduated?

Chapter 10

Review Questions
1. What went wrong in Operation Bughouse?
2. What was the price of the Sergeant's earring? Why didn't the Roughnecks wear them?
3. What did the loss of Buenos Aires mean to Johnnie?
4. What event "really hurt" the Roughnecks? How did it happen?

Thought Questions
1. What does "peace" mean? Why don't people notice casualties that occur in peaceful times?
2. What is the difference between "incidents" and "war"? Is there one?

Chapter 11

Review Questions
1. Why did Johnnie need to straighten things out with Ace? How did they settle the issue?
2. What was difficult about fighting the Bugs?
3. What was Sanctuary like? How was it different from Earth?
4. What advice did Ace give Johnnie? Did he take it?

Thought Questions
1. Is it wise for soldiers to understand why they are fighting? Is it necessary?
2. Heinlein called marriage "a young man's disaster and an old man's comfort." Do you agree?

Chapter 12

Review Questions
1. Whom did Johnnie meet when his ship returned to Base?
2. How was Officer Candidates School different from Boot Camp?
3. What did line of command mean? Why was it important for Johnnie to know?
4. Whose shoulder pips did Johnnie wear?

Thought Questions
1. What is the difference between "man" and a "producing-consuming economic animal"?

2. Is the rescue of one prisoner worth fighting a war? How do you draw those lines?
3. Can you force someone to be socially responsible?

Chapter 13

Review Questions
1. Why did everyone in the Army make the drops?
2. What is the "George" in every outfit?
3. Why did the fleet go to Planet P? What were the goals of Operation Royalty?
4. What happened to the platoon sergeant? Who was he?
5. Did Johnnie graduate? Where was he assigned?

Thought Questions
1. Why do humans instinctively try to rescue other humans? Is this a strength or weakness?
2. What does "home is where the heart is" really mean?

Chapter 14

Review Questions
1. Why couldn't the soldiers use a nova bomb on Klendathu?
2. Who was Johnnie's platoon sergeant?

Thought Questions
1. Throughout the book, Heinlein refers to death in terms of buying and cost. Why? What effect does this have on the way death is portrayed?
2. The book concludes with "To the everlasting glory of the Infantry." What kind of glory is this?

Hand Work
REFINING THE INTRODUCTION

The introduction of an essay is extremely important because it snares the reader's attention, establishes the main argument, and lays out the path the rest of the paper should follow. Writing a good introduction, however, takes practice.

For the following three sample introductions, identify the hook, the thesis, and the road map. Each introduction is missing one piece. Which one? How would you improve these introductions?

Sample 1

Starship Troopers is a book by Robert Heinlein. The book is about a futuristic infantry soldier named Johnnie. Johnnie's questions about the military reflect Heinlein's own questioning during his time in the Navy. This essay will compare experiences in Johnnie's military career with Heinlein's experiences in order to demonstrate the link between Johnnie and Heinlein's thoughts about the military.

Sample 2

In Heinlein's *Starship Troopers*, Hendrick asks, "What's the point in a whole lot of men risking their lives with obsolete weapons when one professor type can do so much more just by pushing a button?" This mentality has become predominant in warfare today.

Sample 3

Although Heinlein's *Starship Troopers* can be read as a fast-paced science fiction novel, it also makes a number of philosophical commentaries on war. This essay will discuss the book's philosophical statements, dividing them according to the characters who present them.

Narrative of the Life of Frederick Douglass
Frederick Douglass

Frederick Augustus Washington Bailey (1818-1895) was born into slavery in Maryland. Although further education was forbidden to him after his mistress taught him the alphabet, he continued to pursue knowledge from other sources. After experiencing the physical cruelties of slavery while working as a field hand on the Eastern Shore, he succeeded in escaping and reached Massachusetts in 1838. Under the name Frederick Douglass, he went on to become a prolific spokesman and writer for the international abolitionist movement. In 1845, he published his autobiography, a book that became famous for its insight into and harsh critique of the slave system.

Chapter 1

Review Questions
1. Who was Douglass' father?
2. When did he see his mother?
3. Why was Douglass' aunt whipped?

Thought Questions
1. Is it worse to have "the means of knowing" withheld than to have knowledge withheld?
2. "God cursed Ham, and therefore American slavery is right." Discuss.

Chapter 2

Review Questions
1. What were the slaves' allowances of food and clothing?
2. Why was the Great House Farm associated with greatness?
3. Why did the slaves sing? What evidence did Douglass cite for this explanation?

Thought Questions
1. Who are "slaves of the political parties"? Do they still exist?
2. Why did songs have so much power to impress people with the horror of slavery?

Chapter 3

Review Questions
1. How did Colonel Lloyd keep the slaves out of the garden?
2. Why was the slave sold to a Georgia trader?
3. Why was it dangerous for a slave to tell the truth?

Thought Questions
1. Do you think kind slave owners existed? Why or why not?
2. "They suppress the truth rather than take the consequences of telling it…In doing so prove themselves a part of the human family." What did Douglass mean? Do you agree?

Chapter 4

Review Questions
1. What kind of person was Mr. Gore?
2. How did he explain Demby's death?
3. Why weren't white people punished for killing blacks?

Chapter 5

Review Questions
1. What did Douglass spend most of his time doing?
2. Where did he go after he left Colonel Lloyd?
3. What were his duties at his new home?

Thought Questions
1. What makes "home" something desirable?
2. In what did Douglass trust? Do you think he had an accurate understanding of God? Discuss.

Chapter 6

Review Questions
1. What made Douglass' new mistress so unusual?
2. Why did her temperament change?
3. What did Douglass learn from his master's warnings?
4. In what way were country slaves and city slaves treated differently?

Thought Questions
1. Why did Douglass call "irresponsible power" a fatal poison? Do you agree?
2. Why do you think Douglass focused on the negative stories about slavery, even when they were the exceptions? Was he right to do so?

Chapter 7

Review Questions
1. What most angered Douglass' mistress?
2. Who became his teachers?
3. What was "The Columbian Orator"? What influence did it have on Douglass?
4. Why didn't Douglass immediately run away?
5. How did he learn to write?

Thought Questions
1. Do people have to practice being cruel? Are they aware that they do so?
2. Why are education and slavery incompatible?
3. Is ignorance bliss? If so, should people be left in ignorance?

Chapter 8

Review Questions
1. Why did Douglass return to the place of his birth?
2. What one experience overwhelmingly caused Douglass to hate slaveholders?
3. Why was Douglass removed from Master Hugh? Where was he taken?

Chapter 9

Review Questions
1. What made Douglass' new master so rare?
2. Did anything change after Captain Auld "experienced religion"?
3. Why was Captain Auld so cruel to Henny?
4. Why was Douglass sent to Edward Covey?

Thought Questions
1. Why do you think people feel the need to use religion to justify cruelty?
2. The theme of blood was very poignant to Douglass. Why? Do you think he was using it to manipulate his audience? If so, do you think he was successful?

Chapter 10

Review Questions
1. Why was Mr. Covey called "the snake"?
2. What was the turning point in Douglass' career as a slave?
3. How did Douglass view the religion of the south?
4. How did Douglass and the others plan to escape? What happened?
5. Why did Douglass leave the shipyard? Why couldn't he press charges against the white men?

Thought Questions
1. Slave owners tried to "disgust the slave with freedom by allowing him to see only the abuse of it." Explain. Do you think this method was effective? Why or why not?
2. Do you think the escapes made possible by decent masters encouraged slaveholders to be cruel?

Chapter 11

Review Questions
1. Why couldn't Douglass write the details of his escape from slavery?
2. What was his complaint against the Underground Railroad?
3. Why did the percentage which Douglass was given from his wages make him angry?
4. How did Douglass earn money? Why did he have to stop?
5. Describe Douglass' emotions on reaching freedom.
6. Why couldn't he work as a caulker in New Bedford?
7. What was the "Liberator"?

Thought Questions
1. Is it better to get the responsibilities or the rights of freedom first?
2. What drove the men of the north to work, if not whipping? What drives you?
3. Do you think Douglass presented a "rose-colored" view of the north? Discuss.

Appendix

Review Questions
1. Was Douglass against all religion? Why or why not?

Thought Questions
1. Douglass said, "Between the Christianity of this land, and the Christianity of Christ, I recognize the widest possible difference." What is the Christianity of America like today?
2. Do Christians still "love the heathen on the other side of the world" and "despise… the heathen at their own doors"? Why do you think this happens?
3. Has Douglass' sacred cause been accomplished yet?

Brain Work
DEVELOPING A THESIS

In order to choose a thesis, you must a) read the book, and b) think about it. While a good thesis should be original and interesting, it must be backed up by the book about which you are writing. Keep in mind also that a good thesis may be provocative or harsh — as long as it does not misrepresent the book.

After reading Frederick Douglass' autobiography, look at the following sample theses. Decide which ones are supported by the book and which are not. Give a brief explanation for each of your decisions.

1. In his autobiography, F. Douglass presents an incomplete picture of slavery by only focusing on the negative experiences and stories.

2. Douglass' anti-slavery efforts were individualistic, not cooperative. In his autobiography, his unwillingness to name those who helped him escape from slavery demonstrates this egotistical tendency.

3. It can be argued that F. Douglass was directing his autobiography toward two audiences: the abolitionists of the north, whom he wanted to fill with guilt and rage, and the slaves in the south, whom he wanted to give a desire for freedom.

4. Although Douglass railed against the hypocrisy of Southern religion, his final comments on Christianity indicate that some of the white Christians' teachings had a positive effect on his life.

5. If Douglass' discussion of slavery is more cynical than that of other writers, it is because his experience with slavery was longer and harsher than the experiences of many who opposed slavery.

Up from Slavery
Booker T. Washington

Booker Taliaferro Washington (1856-1915) was the son of a white father and a black slave mother in Virginia. He was freed in 1865, after the conclusion of the Civil War, and he and his family moved to West Virginia to work in the coal mines. Washington later left to attend the Hampton Institute in Virginia, and in 1881, he founded the Tuskegee Institute in Alabama on a model of vocational training as well as intellectual study. A savvy politician as well an educator, Washington became a prominent orator and writer on race relations across the United States. He published his autobiography, *Up from Slavery*, in 1901. The book chronicles his life-long efforts to uproot prejudice and ignorance.

Chapter 1 – A Slave Among Slaves

Review Questions
1. Why were Washington's early surroundings so miserable and desolate?
2. What did Washington believe to be the central issue?
3. What was young Washington's greatest ordeal? How did his brother John help?
4. What did freedom mean to the slaves?

Thought Questions
1. Do circumstances affect the morality of an action, as Washington claimed for his mother's theft?
2. Why is it important for children to be able to play?
3. Did Washington hate slavery? Explain. Is it possible to love someone who enslaves you?

Chapter 2 – Boyhood Days

Review Questions
1. On what two things did the slaves agree?
2. Why did Washington and his family move to West Virginia?
3. How did he learn to read? Why didn't he attend the new school?
4. How did Washington get his name?

   5. Why did he dislike working in the coal mines?

Thought Questions
   1. Washington's mother refused to go into debt, and she refused to seem to be what she was not. Do these two principles have anything in common? If so, what?
   2. "The Negro youth starts out with the presumption against him." Is this true today?
   3. Is it a human law that merit is always recognized and rewarded in the long run?

Chapter 3 – The Struggle for an Education

Review Questions
   1. Where did Washington want to attend school? How did he get there?
   2. What was his entrance exam?
   3. Who made the greatest impression on Washington? Why?
   4. How did Washington earn his board and tuition?

Thought Questions
   1. Where does bitterness come from? How can you avoid becoming bitter?
   2. "There is no education which one can get from books and costly apparatus that is equal to that which can be gotten from contact with great men and women." Do you agree?

Chapter 4 – Helping Others

Review Questions
   1. What did Washington do over the summer?
   2. Why were labor strikes unprofitable for mining workers?
   3. What besides books did Washington teach at Malden?
   4. What gift did Washington give his brother John?

Thought Questions
   1. Why do you think Miss Mackie delighted in menial service?
   2. What makes the toothbrush such an influential civilizer?
   3. What does it mean to "give back" to your community? Why is it important?

Chapter 5 – The Reconstruction Period

Review Questions
   1. What were the two desires of colored people during Reconstruction?
   2. Why was the surge of new teachers and pastors a bad thing?
   3. What, according to Washington, was wrong with Reconstruction policies?
   4. What concerned Washington about the large class of colored people in D.C.?

Thought Questions
   1. Why is it dangerous to look to a central government for everything?
   2. Which should come first, freedom or education? Defend your answer.
   3. Can any law apply "without opportunity for double dealing or evasion"? Why or why not?

Chapter 6 – Black Race and Red Race

Review Questions
   1. What made Hampton Institute unique?

2. What happened when Washington took the young Indian man to Washington?
3. What was the purpose of the night school?

Thought Questions
1. Is political success a selfish kind of success?
2. "No white American ever thinks that any other race is wholly civilized until he wears the white man's clothes, eats the white man's food, speaks the white man's language, and professes the white man's religion." Is this true?
3. Why didn't people recognize the hypocrisy of their racial hierarchies?

Chapter 7 – Early Days at Tuskegee

Review Questions
1. What new opportunity opened for Washington?
2. What factors made Tuskegee a good site for a school? What factors made it difficult?
3. What was the mentality of the country people?

Chapter 8 – Teaching School in a Stable and a Hen-House

Review Questions
1. Why did some white residents fear and resent the new school?
2. Who was Olivia Davidson?
3. Why did most black people want an education?
4. Where did the Institute become established? How did Washington repay the loan?

Thought Questions
1. Why is it important to know and practice hygiene? Where did you learn these things?
2. Is manual labor demeaning? Why is it viewed that way?

Chapter 9 – Anxious Days and Sleepless Nights

Review Questions
1. How was Christmas celebrated in Tuskegee?
2. Why did Washington want to make the school a part of the community?
3. What made Washington's burden (making the school succeed) doubly heavy?

Thought Questions
1. What is the "proper" observance of Christmas? Discuss.
2. Why is it embarrassing to ask for monetary support? How is support different from charity?

Chapter 10 – A Harder Task than Making Bricks Without Straw

Review Questions
1. Why did Washington want the students to construct their own buildings?
2. Why was Washington glad for the problems with the dining facilities?

Thought Questions
1. Are economic relations a good model for relations between races? Between nations?
2. "The visible…goes a long way in softening prejudices." Is this always true?
3. Can patience, wisdom, and honest effort solve all problems?

Chapter 11 – Making Their Beds Before They Could Lie on Them

Review Questions
1. What did Washington learn about General Armstrong on the general's visit to Tuskegee?
2. Why was cleanliness emphasized at the Tuskegee Institute?

Thought Questions
1. Why do you think Washington earned so much respect from black and white people alike?
2. Would open communication, trust, and responsibility decrease the number of labor strikes?

Chapter 12 – Raising Money

Review Questions
1. What were Washington's rules for fundraising?
2. Why did Washington insist that he was not a beggar? What are "strict business methods"?
3. Did most of the funds for the Institute come from large or small donations?

Thought Questions
1. General Armstrong was described as, "Too big to be little, too good to be mean." Explain.
2. What does it mean to, "Give them an idea for every word"?
3. Is the world "growing in the direction of giving"? Support your answer.

Chapter 13 – Two Thousand Miles for a Five-Minute Speech

Review Questions
1. Why did Washington establish a night-school? What made it a severe test of students' worth?
2. When did Washington start his public speaking career?
3. Where was the best place to criticize the South?
4. Why did Washington travel so far for such a short speech in Atlanta?
5. How did Washington achieve a national reputation?

Thought Questions
1. Does mastery of one area of work tend to lead to motivation or complacency?
2. In public speaking, how is the audience different from the individuals that compose it? Is it?

Chapter 14 – The Atlanta Exposition Address

Review Questions
1. According to Washington's address, what was the greatest danger for the black race?
2. What impressed Washington about President Cleveland?
3. Why did some colored people later react badly to the speech?
4. What did Washington think about the political conditions/future of his race?

Thought Questions
1. Explain the "cast down your bucket" illustration that Washington used.
2. Why do you think Washington's address had such widespread positive effect?

3. Are "slow but sure influences" always the best way to effect change?

Chapter 15 – The Secret of Success in Public Speaking

Review Questions
1. What was Washington's compensation for the nervousness he felt before speaking?
2. At the Jubilee week address, how did Washington appeal to the consciences of white Americans?
3. Who were the "cranks" and why did Washington dread them?

Thought Questions
1. Can someone be an effective public speaker without possessing a heartfelt message?
2. How can you retain mastery over your work without being driven by it?

Chapter 16 – Europe

Review Questions
1. What trades did Washington's children pursue?
2. Why did Washington go to Europe? Why did he hesitate to go?
3. In what ways were the French ahead of/behind the American Negro?
4. How were the English superior to the Americans?

Thought Questions
1. Is it fair to have to do something exceptional in order to be recognized, if others are recognized for mediocre achievement?
2. Do you think a fixed system of servitude or one that is upwardly mobile is to be preferred?
3. Was Washington a humble man? Why or why not?

Chapter 17 – Last Words

Review Questions
1. Why did Washington travel to Harvard?
2. What, according to Washington, is the one standard by which to measure success?
3. What was Washington's secret goal in regards to Tuskegee Institute? When was it realized?
4. What are the three goals of an industrial education?

Thought Questions
1. What do you think is the purpose of fame? Does it serve a purpose?
2. Does generosity or wise giving have greater value? Why?
3. In your opinion, what was Washington's most lasting contribution to race relations?

Hand Work
REVISING THE CONCLUSION

Imagine you are writing a short paper about Booker T. Washington's suggestions for dealing with the effects of slavery. Your introduction is below. Assume that you have written one paragraph about each of the main points in the road map. Now write a conclusion that sums up the main argument in a way that is memorable, concise, and gives a sense of finality (i.e., does not introduce new points). Use the examples below as models. Hint: Start by identifying the thesis and road map in the introduction.

Introduction

"I had the feeling that it was cruelly wrong in the central government, at the beginning of our freedom, to fail to make some provision for the general education of our people" (Washington 50). In his autobiography *Up from Slavery*, Booker T. Washington proposes that the best way to deal with the effects of slavery is a combination of freedom from bitterness and vocational education. These two beliefs can best be examined as they appear in the principles behind Washington's Tuskegee Institute.

Memorable

1. Washington's focus on education is an interesting and different way to deal with the effects of slavery. (Needs work)

2. Washington's focus on vocational education as the foundation of a productive society offered an alternative to pictures of ex-slaves as helpless victims. (Better)

Concise

1. Washington encouraged ex-slaves to put aside their bitterness and focus on getting a good education that would give them the skills to be productive members of society who proved their merits instead of focusing on the ways they had been disadvantaged. (Needs work)

2. Washington encouraged ex-slaves not to dwell in bitterness and self-pity, but to prove themselves worthy members of society by getting a good vocational education. (Better)

Final

1. Washington's perspectives on slavery, while enlightening, probably stemmed from his personal experience with slavery, which was not especially severe. (Needs work)

2. Although Washington's perspectives on slavery stemmed from his personal experiences, his work nonetheless has had a significant impact on the continuing struggle for racial equality. (Better)

The Glass Menagerie
Tennessee Williams

Thomas Lanier Williams III (1911-1983) began to write in part because he spent much of his childhood as an invalid. Born in Mississippi, Williams moved to St. Louis with his family during the Great Depression and remained in the Midwest to attend school. He was given the name "Tennessee" by his college friends in recognition of his deep southern accent. As an adult, Williams moved to New Orleans, where he would later set one of his most famous plays, *A Streetcar Named Desire*, which won a Pulitzer Prize in 1948. Williams won the Pulitzer again in 1955 with *Cat on a Hot Tin Roof*. *The Glass Menagerie*, a deeply personal play, was his first success. It was published in 1944 after being performed in Chicago and on Broadway.

Scene 1

Review Questions
1. Who are the characters in the play?
2. What is a "memory play"?
3. What story did Amanda like to tell?

Thought Questions
1. How is the play different because it is a "memory play"?
2. What is the mood of the play?

Scene 2

Review Questions
1. In what way had Laura deceived her mother? Why had she deceived her?
2. Which boy had Laura liked? Why had he called her "Blue Roses"?
3. Why didn't Laura think she could marry?

Thought Questions
1. Have you ever quit something because of fear or humiliation? Has the experience had any lasting impact on you? If so, what?
2. Was Amanda's final comment, that Laura's father had charm, a compliment or a complaint?

Scene 3

Review Questions

   1. What goal began to occupy Amanda's mind?

   2. Why were Tom and Amanda fighting?

   3. What prevented Tom from leaving?

Thought Questions

   1. What didn't Amanda understand about Tom? What didn't he understand about her?

   2. In your opinion, what were Tom's feelings toward Amanda? Toward Laura?

Scene 4

Review Questions

   1. What did Laura ask Tom to do?

   2. Who made the first step toward reconciliation?

   3. Why did Amanda want to talk about Laura? What did she ask Tom to do?

Thought Questions

   1. Why do some people nag? What is the best way to respond to nagging?

   2. Why did Tom spend so much time at the movies? Did he?

   3. Can you respect someone without understanding them?

   4. Is it a bad thing to follow your instincts? Why or why not?

Scene 5

Review Questions

   1. What news did Tom give Amanda?

   2. What was Amanda's biggest concern about prospective gentlemen callers?

   3. Why had Amanda married her husband even though he drank?

Thought Questions

   1. Does the past "turn into everlasting regret if you don't plan for it"? Discuss.

   2. Why did Tom say Laura was very different from other girls? Was she peculiar? Explain.

Scene 6

Review Questions

   1. How did Tom and Jim know each other?

   2. Why was Laura upset when she found out who was the gentleman caller?

   3. Why did Jim recommend taking a public speaking course?

   4. Where did Tom plan to move?

Thought Questions

   1. Why was Laura so afraid to answer the door?

   2. What is the difference between manual laborers and executives? Is there one?

   3. Do people today "go to the movies instead of moving"? If so, why?

Scene 7

Review Questions

   1. Why did the lights go out?

2. How did Laura and Jim end up alone together?
3. What had Laura done since high school?
4. According to Jim, what was Laura's problem?
5. What happened when Jim asked Laura to dance?
6. What mistake had Tom made?
7. Why did Jim leave?
8. Why did Tom leave? What pursued him?

Thought Questions
1. What is the difference between being disappointed and being discouraged?
2. "Time is the longest distance between two places." Explain.
3. Why did Tom tell Laura to "blow out [her] candles"?
4. What does it mean, "The world is lit by lightning"? Compare lightning and candle-light. How does this comparison relate to the rest of the play?

Brain Work
BUILDING AN ARGUMENT

Building an argument is challenging, and it is easy to make logical errors when writing about literature. Below is a list of common fallacies in the arguments of literary essays. Study these fallacies, and then for each practice argument, decide which fallacy has been committed.

Oversimplification (OS) – The argument fails to take into account pertinent factors or ignores the complexity of a situation. For example, in a book where a character struggles to understand his entire family, it would be an oversimplification to say that one incident with a sibling was the cause of all of the main character's problems.

No textual support (NTS) – This kind of argument is exaggerated or completely made up. It may be related to the book, but it is not suggested by the book. In a story about a girl trying to come to terms with the Holocaust, it would be a fallacy to argue that her father must have been a Communist because the family opposed Hitler (unless this link was directly suggested).

Already apparent (AA) – This is the opposite of the NTS fallacy. A thesis should draw out a subtle theme or development from the book. If the author clearly states that your thesis is true, then there is little point in writing the essay, except as a book report.

Missing link (ML) – In this fallacy, the general logic of the argument may be sound, but the argument is missing a step or making an unsupported assumption. A mathematical example would be if you were told that A = B and C = D and you jumped to the conclusion that A = D. This argument would be invalid unless you could prove that B = C.

Contextual misunderstanding (CM) – This fallacy is subtle. Although classic works of literature can be read and appreciated by multiple generations, you must remember that each author wrote in a specific time in history. Words and customs from that society should be read as they were understood in that context, even if they now have a different meaning. For example, in the past, marriage customs have varied greatly. It would be a fallacy to argue that a sixteenth century couple was not truly married because they did not receive marriage certificates.

Practice

Each of these arguments commits a literary fallacy. List the fallacy, and then explain why you think it has been committed. There may be more than one way to categorize the fallacy in each argument.

1. *The Glass Menagerie* is narrated by Tom in the future. All of the other characters appear only in the past. This indicates that Tom is the only one who is still alive. Since Tom is the only one still alive, his understanding of the world must have been the only valid one.

2. In *The Glass Menagerie*, Laura's humiliation at the typing school was the final humiliation that made her peculiar. If she had met Jim before dropping out of the business school the play might have ended very differently.

3. When Jim, of *The Glass Menagerie*, asked Laura to waltz with him, he was stepping back into her slower, out-of-date world. In doing so, he broke the glass unicorn. This showed that Jim could not fit into Laura's world.

4. Jim liked to talk about becoming a sailor. When he said he was "going to the movies," he was actually contracting work aboard a ship. His father, who left before him, owned the ship and encouraged Jim to work with him.

To Kill a Mockingbird

Harper Lee

Nelle Harper Lee (1926-2016) is an Alabama native and a descendent of General Robert E. Lee. After beginning her education in law, she turned to literature instead and moved to New York to pursue her writing. Lee wrote only one book: *To Kill a Mockingbird*, which was published in 1960, and won a Pulitzer Prize in 1961. After finishing the novel, Lee returned to the South and did not publish again. *To Kill a Mockingbird* is set in the 1930s, and shows the effects of racial prejudice on a small Alabama town through the eyes of a young girl named Jean Louise Finch.

Chapter 1

Review Questions
1. Where did Atticus and his family live?
2. Who was Calpurnia?
3. Why did she live with the Finches?
4. Why was Dill spending the summer with Miss Rachel?
5. Who was Boo Radley, and why did Dill want him to come out?

Thought Questions
1. Why are the consequences sometimes harsher for those who plead "not guilty"?
2. What is the difference between respect and fear? Is it a big difference?

Chapter 2

Review Questions
1. What activity consoled Scout when Dill left?
2. Why didn't Walter Cunningham have a lunch?

Thought Questions
1. Why do you think Miss Caroline was upset that Scout could already read?
2. "Until I feared I would lose it, I never loved to read." Why?

Chapter 3

Review Questions

1. Why did Jem invite Walter to dinner?
2. What did Scout do to earn Calpurnia's displeasure?
3. Why did Miss Caroline send Burris Ewell home?

Thought Questions

1. Do the children at the school seem like first graders to you? What makes some children grow up faster than others?
2. "Sometimes it is better to bend the law a little in special cases." Do you agree?
3. Is a compromise the same thing as bending the law? Why or why not?

Chapter 4

Review Questions

1. What did Scout find by the Radley house?
2. Who left the gifts?
3. How did Scout end up next to the Radleys' steps?

Thought Questions

1. In your opinion, why didn't Atticus want the children to act out the Radleys' life story?
2. Is curiosity ever wrong? When does it become wrong?

Chapter 5

Review Questions

1. Why did Scout begin to spend more time with Miss Maudie?
2. Why, according to Miss Maudie, did Boo Radley not want to leave his house?
3. What message did Jem and Dill want to send to Boo?
4. How did they attempt to get it to him?

Thought Questions

1. What is wrong with "worrying about the next world" until you "never [learn] to live in this one"?
2. Were Dill, Jem, and Scout cruel to Boo Radley?
3. Can you be cruel unintentionally? Discuss.

Chapter 6

Review Questions

1. What did the children do on Dill's last night?
2. Who caught them?
3. What did Jem lose?

Thought Questions

1. Why did it mean so much to Jem that Atticus had never whipped him?
2. Did Scout and Jem respect their father? Why or why not?

Chapter 7

Review Questions

1. What was unusual about Jem's pants after the night at the Radleys'?
2. What treasures did Jem and Scout find in the knot-hole?
3. Why couldn't Jem and Scout deliver their note as planned?

Thought Questions
1. Why do you think Nathan Radley put cement in the tree?
2. Why did Jem cry when Mr. Radley filled in the knot-hole?
3. Why do you think Boo gave the children gifts?
4. Why didn't Nathan want him to do it?

Chapter 8

Review Questions
1. Why did Scout think the world was ending?
2. How did Jem make a snowman?
3. Why did Atticus tell him to change it?
4. What happened to Miss Maudie?
5. What did Boo give Scout?

Thought Questions
1. Is it strange that Miss Maudie wasn't upset about her house? Why or why not?

Chapter 9

Review Questions
1. Why did Scout almost fight Cecil Jacobs?
2. Why did Atticus choose to defend Tom Robinson?
3. What did Atticus ask Scout to do?
4. What made Christmas unpleasant for Scout?
5. Why did Scout fight with Francis?

Thought Questions
1. "Every lawyer gets at least one case in his lifetime that affects him personally." Why?
2. Why would Atticus be unable to tell Scout and Jem what to do if he refused to defend Tom?
3. Why was Atticus "licked a hundred years before [he] started"?
4. Do you think Uncle Jack was right to discipline Scout?
5. Were Atticus's methods of discipline good? Were they effective?

Chapter 10

Review Questions
1. Why was it a sin to kill a mockingbird?
2. What was wrong with Mr. Johnson's dog?
3. How did Atticus earn the respect of his children?

Thought Questions
1. What does a father today have to do in order to be respected by his children?
2. "People in their right minds never take pride in their talents." Discuss. Do you agree?
3. What does it mean to be a gentleman? A lady?

Chapter 11

Review Questions
1. Why was Mrs. Dubose so unpleasant?
2. What did Jem do to her on the way home? Why?
3. What did Mrs. Dubose want Jem to do?
4. What caused Mrs. Dubose's fits?

Thought Questions
1. "One thing that doesn't abide by majority rule is a person's conscience." Is this true?
2. What is real courage?

Chapter 12

Review Questions
1. Why didn't Dill come for the summer?
2. Why did the children go to Calpurnia's church? How was it different?
3. Of what was Tom Robinson accused?
4. Why didn't Cal talk "proper" at her church?
5. Who was waiting at the house when they returned?

Thought Questions
1. Do different denominations of the Christian church forget, "It's the same God"? Discuss.
2. What is the "Impurity of Women" doctrine? What is the basis for it?

Chapter 13

Review Questions
1. Why had Aunt Alexandra come?
2. What was Maycomb's primary reason for existence?

Thought Questions
1. Do families have "streaks," as Aunt Alexandra would say?
2. What did Atticus try to do that only a woman could do?

Chapter 14

Review Questions
1. How did Atticus define rape?
2. Why did Aunt Alexandra want Calpurnia to leave?
3. What was Scout's "snake"?
4. Why had Dill left home?

Thought Questions
1. Should parents answer all of their children's questions?
2. If not, where should they draw the line?
3. Why did Scout feel better after fighting with Jem?

Chapter 15

Review Questions
1. Why did Heck Tate visit Atticus?

   2. Where did Atticus go with the light bulb and extension cord?

   3. Why did the children follow?

   4. What did the group of men want at the jail?

   5. What made them leave?

Thought Questions

   1. Why did Jem's exclamation about the phone disrupt the tension with Heck Tate?

   2. Why did Scout's comments to Mr. Cunningham make the men leave?

   3. What did these two situations, and their results, have in common?

Chapter 16

Review Questions

   1. Why did so many people go into town?

   2. Where did the children sit to watch the trial?

Thought Questions

   1. "A mob is always made up of people." Explain. Do you agree?

   2. "Once you have a drop of Negro blood, that makes you all black." What are some weaknesses in this argument? What are the consequences if it is true?

   3. Scout was confused because the townspeople were angry at Atticus for defending Tom Robinson. In her opinion, being appointed to defend someone meant you should defend that person. Was Scout confused, or were the townspeople confused?

Chapter 17

Review Questions

   1. What two main things did Atticus ask Heck Tate?

   2. Why did it matter which side of Mayella's face had been beaten?

   3. Why hadn't Mr. Ewell run for a doctor?

   4. Why did Atticus want to know if Mr. Ewell was literate?

Thought Questions

   1. Why did Mr. Ewell's accusation, however crude, have such an impact on the audience?

   2. Why shouldn't a lawyer ask a question if he/she doesn't know the answer? Are trials scripted?

Chapter 18

Review Questions

   1. Why was Mayella afraid of Atticus?

   2. Why did Atticus ask Mayella so many seemingly pointless questions?

   3. What was odd about Tom Robinson?

Thought Questions

   1. What effect do you think Mayella's final outburst had on the jury? Why?

Chapter 19

Review Questions

   1. Who was Atticus's witness?

2. What had been so unusual to Tom about the night of November 21?

3. Why had Tom's predicament been so subtly complicated?

4. How did Tom's version of the story differ from Mayella's? How did Tom explain the difference?

Thought Questions

1. Why was it wrong for Tom to pity Mayella?

2. Why was Dill so upset? Do you think Mr. Gilmer treated Tom unfairly?

Chapter 20

Review Questions

1. What was Mr. Raymond's secret? Why did he keep it a secret?

2. Why did Atticus say Mayella was motivated by guilt?

3. Who entered the courtroom as Atticus finished speaking?

Thought Questions

1. Are all men created equal? In what sense?

2. Was Atticus an idealist "to believe firmly in the integrity of our courts and in the jury system"?

3. Are courts today the "great levelers"?

Chapter 21

Review Questions

1. Why did Calpurnia come to the courtroom?

2. Who did Jem believe had won the case? What was the jury's verdict?

3. How did the Negroes show respect for Atticus?

Chapter 22

Review Questions

1. Who sent Atticus all the food?

2. Why did Miss Maudie call Judge Taylor Tom Robinson's ally?

3. What did Mr. Ewell do to Atticus?

Thought Questions

1. Why was Tom convicted?

2. "Christian judges an' lawyers [can't] make up for heathen juries." Why do we have a jury system?

Chapter 23

Review Questions

1. Why was Atticus willing for Bob Ewell to threaten him?

2. What had come between the jurors and reason?

3. Why hadn't Miss Maudie ever sat on a jury?

4. Who did Atticus believe had been unwilling to convict Tom? Why?

Thought Questions

1. Should only judges be allowed to give out capital punishment sentences? Why or why not?

2. What is *background*? Does it have real value?

3. Is there more than one kind of people?
4. Why do you think Boo Radley stayed inside?

Chapter 24

Review Questions
1. What did Mrs. Merriweather hope would blow over?
2. Why did Miss Maudie ask, "His food doesn't stick going down, does it?"?
3. What happened to Tom Robinson when he arrived at the prison camp?
4. What news did Atticus bring?
5. According to Miss Maudie, how had the town paid tribute to Atticus?

Chapter 25

Review Questions
1. How did Maycomb interpret the news?
2. How did Mr. Ewell react?

Thought Questions
1. Why do you think Tom tried to run?
2. Why did Mr. Underwood liken Tom's death to the killing of a cripple?

Chapter 26

Review Questions
1. Why did the people re-elect Atticus to the legislature if they hated him?
2. What current event did Cecil Jacobs report to the class?

Thought Questions
1. Are there any similarities between the Holocaust and Tom Robinson's trial? Discuss.
2. What is the irony in the children's anger about the persecution of Jews?
3. Are there any situations today in which Americans are similarly hypocritical? Explain.
4. Why didn't Jem want to hear about the courthouse?

Chapter 27

Review Questions
1. What three unusual things happened in Maycomb? How were they related?
2. Why did Mr. Ewell hold a grudge?
3. In what way had Halloween gone too far the previous year?
4. How was Halloween different this year?
5. What was Scout's role in the pageant?

Thought Questions
1. Which is worse, to be called a fool or a liar? Why?
2. What do you think Mr. Ewell hoped to achieve through the court case?
3. Why did he fail?

Chapter 28

Review Questions
1. What frightened the children on the way to the pageant?

2. How did Scout mess up the pageant?
3. What happened on the way home?
4. What was wrong with Jem?
5. What did Mr. Tate find?

Chapter 29

Review Questions

1. Who had rescued Scout and Jem?

Thought Questions

1. Was Mr. Ewell a coward?

Chapter 30

Review Questions

1. What did Atticus think had happened to Bob Ewell?
2. What was Mr. Tate's explanation?
3. Who killed Bob Ewell?

Thought Questions

1. Why didn't Atticus want the story hushed up?
2. Why did Mr. Tate lie?
3. "I can't live one way in town and another way in my home." Why not? Explain.
4. Why did Mr. Tate tell Atticus to "let the dead bury the dead"? What did he mean?
5. How would telling the truth be like shooting a mockingbird?

Chapter 31

Review Questions

1. What did Boo Radley want to do before he left?
2. What did he ask Scout to do?

Thought Questions

1. How did Scout's perspective change when she stood on the Radleys' porch?
2. Are most people pretty nice "when you finally see them"?

Hand Work
PROOFREADING

1. For the first paragraph, your job is to eliminate all unnecessary words and phrases, making it clearer and more concise. Read the paragraph aloud. If a sentence is difficult to read, you can probably cut out some words. If a sentence or expression is repetitive, cross out the unneeded words. Your goal is to make the paragraph concise and smooth without changing its meaning.

   Paragraph 1

   Although the dramatic scene in *To Kill a Mockingbird* takes place in the courtroom, the true test of justice occurs when Atticus and Heck Tate decide whether or not to condemn Bob Ewell's murderer. Atticus is a lawyer so he thinks justice is objective. Heck Tate is familiar with the people of Maycomb County, so he thinks it is more important to look at the way people react to issues. Atticus' point of view centers on the importance of the law and objective justice; Heck Tate's ideas are built on popular response. The confrontation raises an interesting, but unanswered question: is justice really just if it fails to take the human factor into account? Harper Lee does not provide an answer.

2. The second paragraph contains a number of grammatical and spelling errors. Look for shifts in verb tense, subjects and verbs or nouns and pronouns that do not agree in number, misspelled words, and incorrect usage of commonly confused words (where and were, for example). Other errors may include capitalization and punctuation problems, fragments, and run-on sentences. Before you start this exercise, consider finding a grammar book and refreshing your memory on common mistakes and how to fix them.

   Paragraph 2

   Children tend to seeing the world in terms of black and white. Adults, by contrast, usually added the shades of gray that make life much more complacated. *To kill a mockingbird* are told from the perspictive of a child, making it the perfect setting for a struggle between black-and-white and gray as scout is forced to revaluate the meaning of abstract ideas like justice, fairness, honer and honesty. Because their is no easy definition for any of these terms the book is as much a reminder that the reader is still a child in understanding. As they were a cronicle of scout's increasing matureity.

Walden
Henry D. Thoreau

Henry David Thoreau (1817-1862) was born in Concord, Massachusetts, where he spent most of his adult life. When he graduated from Harvard, he struggled to find work, and after several teaching attempts, he became a handyman for philosopher Ralph Waldo Emerson. In 1845, Emerson gave Thoreau permission to live on a piece of land near Walden Pond as an economic and social experiment in simple living and transcendental thought. During his two years at the pond, Thoreau began work on *Walden*, a book originally written in response to questions about what he was doing. He published the book in 1854. After concluding his experiment at Walden Pond, Thoreau continued to travel and write about a range of social issues.

Chapter 1 – Economy

Review Questions

1. Where did Thoreau live while he wrote this book? Why did he write it? For whom?
2. Why did Thoreau call people frivolous?
3. Why would it be advantageous to live a primitive, frontier life?
4. What did Thoreau mean by "necessaries of life"? What are these necessities?
5. What does it mean to be a philosopher?
6. Did most people Thoreau observed own their own homes?
7. What makes some people "needlessly poor"?
8. What kind of house did Thoreau build? What was the total cost of building it?
9. What did Thoreau think about education? What was its purpose? What were its flaws?
10. How did Thoreau raise money for his farm? Was it profitable in economic terms?
11. What sacrament did Thoreau praise, and why?
12. How much of the year did Thoreau work?
13. What is wrong with philanthropy, according to Thoreau?

Thought Questions

1. Is property a gift or a curse? Explain.
2. Thoreau said, "The mass of men lead lives of quiet desperation." Do you agree?
3. Do the old have any important advice to give the young?

4. How far would men retain their relative ranks if they were divested of their clothes?
5. Is civilization a real advance in the condition of man? Why or why not?
6. Why don't people choose to live simply?
7. Why do houses have doors (windows) (cellars) (garrets)?
8. Thoreau said he "brags for humanity" rather than for himself. Explain.
9. What is the difference between living life and playing or studying it?
10. Do inventions generally arise to serve a need or does a need arise to serve the invention?

Chapter 2 – Where I Lived, and What I Lived For

Review Questions
1. What was Thoreau's position on owning land?
2. How well-built was Thoreau's house?
3. What was the real value of the lake, or of having water nearby?
4. What time of day did Thoreau do his best work?
5. According to Thoreau, what were the "sleepers" under the railroad?
6. Why did he say people come when they think there is a fire?
7. What were Thoreau's thoughts on the post office?
8. Why did Thoreau say children may be wiser than adults?
9. How did Thoreau believe intellect should be used?

Thought Questions
1. Thoreau claimed that the poet gets more out of the farm than the farmer. Explain. Do you agree?
2. "Little is to be expected of that day, if it can be called a day, to which we are not awakened by our Genius, but by the mechanical nudgings of some servitor." Which one awakens you?
3. Can you "reduce life to the lowest terms"? If so, what are they?
4. Are news and gossip the same thing? Why or why not?
5. What is the difference between appearance and being?
6. Is there a reality beneath opinion, prejudice, tradition, delusion, and appearance? How do you know? How did Thoreau know?

Chapter 3 – Reading

Review Questions
1. What two occupations interest everyone?
2. Why should individuals study dead/ancient languages?
3. What did Thoreau include in the meaning of the word "illiterate"?

Thought Questions
1. Do you read "shallow" books? If so, why? Is there any harm in "easy reading"?
2. Are the language of literature and the common language still separate in English?
3. Since Thoreau's time, many of the great classic works of literature have been translated. Does this mean we are now able, with their help, "to scale heaven"?
4. "Instead of noblemen, let us have noble villages of men." What is the difference?

Chapter 4 – Sounds

Review Questions
1. Did Thoreau place more value on work or contemplation? Why?

2. What linked Thoreau to society?
3. What did it mean to do things "railroad fashion"?
4. What shipments passed in and out of Concord?
5. What did Thoreau like about the owls?

Chapter 5 – Solitude

Review Questions
1. How did Thoreau know when visitors had been at his house?
2. Was Thoreau ever lonely?
3. What did Thoreau believe about spirituality in the world?
4. Who were Thoreau's two closest companions?

Thought Questions
1. "They plainly fished much more in the Walden Pond of their own natures, and baited their hooks with darkness." Explain.
2. Are men still afraid of the dark? Why?
3. What makes something solitary? When does solitude become troublesome?

Chapter 6 – Visitors

Review Questions
1. What was Thoreau's one complaint about the small size of his house?
2. What advice did Thoreau give in terms of hospitality?
3. Why did Thoreau like the Canadian wood chopper?
4. How did the woodman defend the use of money? What made it a good defense?

Thought Questions
1. Do you agree with Thoreau about maintaining distance between speakers? Why?
2. Is it easy to break old customs? What are the probable consequences of trying?
3. Thoreau asked, "What danger is there if you don't think of any?" Is this true?

Chapter 7 – The Bean-Field

Review Questions
1. Why did Thoreau call his a "half-cultivated" field?
2. Did Thoreau make a profit from his beans?
3. Why, according to Thoreau, did farmers continue to sow beans? What crops did he propose?

Thought Questions
1. What is the moral value of gardening? Is there one?
2. Thoreau said farmers should relinquish their anxieties and claims to their produce. How does this compare to Jesus' words in Matthew, at the end of chapter six?

Chapter 8 – The Village

Review Questions
1. What were the vitals of the village?
2. Why was it a valuable experience to be lost in the woods?
3. Why was Thoreau jailed on one of his visits to town?

Thought Questions
1. Do you keep your doors locked at night? Why or why not?
2. Do robberies only take place when there is an unequal distribution of wealth? Explain.

Chapter 9 – The Ponds

Review Questions
1. Briefly describe Walden Pond.
2. What did Thoreau believe made the path around the pond?
3. What was the purpose of the rise and fall of the pond waters?
4. How had the shore of the pond been paved?
5. Why did Thoreau compare the trains to the Trojan horse?
6. Why did Thoreau protest the name of Flint's Pond? What name did he propose?

Thought Questions
1. Thoreau referred to God as creator. Does this fit with his other comments about God? Explain.
2. Thoreau says ponds are "more beautiful than our lives…more transparent than our characters." Is his praise warranted? Is it appropriate?

Chapter 10 – Baker Farm

Review Questions
1. Who was John Field?
2. What kept the Fields from living as Thoreau did?

Thought Questions
1. Thoreau said the only true America was a country where men were free to live simply and were not required to pay for the superfluities of the government. Would today's America qualify?
2. Are people born to be poor? Explain.

Chapter 11 – Higher Laws

Review Questions
1. Why did Thoreau call hunting and fishing a valuable part of an individual's education?
2. Why did he think vegetarianism was practical?
3. What was his position on alcohol?

Thought Questions
1. Thoreau said he loved "the wild not less than the good." Explain. Do you agree?
2. Do purity and chastity allow individuals to draw closer to God? Why or why not?
3. Is there any point to Christianity if it does not translate into purer action?
4. "We are all sculptors and painters…our material is our own flesh and blood." Do you agree?

Chapter 12 – Brute Neighbors

Review Questions
1. What were Thoreau's hens and chickens?
2. What battle did he witness?

3. What was the "winged cat"?

Thought Questions
1. Why do you think Thoreau felt the need to relate these animal stories to his reader?

Chapter 13 – House-Warming

Review Questions
1. Why did Thoreau call the northeast side of Walden the "fireside of the pond"?
2. When did Thoreau begin to inhabit his house, by his reckoning?
3. Why was he interested in the first ice before the general freeze?
4. How did the stumps from the bean-field warm Thoreau twice?
5. What did Thoreau call his "housekeeper"?
6. Why did he regret getting a cook stove?

Thought Questions
1. Give an example of "sayings which men love to repeat whether they are true or not."
2. When you are a guest, what makes you feel at home? Do you agree with Thoreau's analysis?
3. For someone who loved solitude, Thoreau argued strongly in favor of companionship. Is this contradictory? Why or why not?

Chapter 14 – Former Inhabitants; and Winter Visitors

Review Questions
1. Who were the old occupants of the woods? Why had they left?
2. What had happened to Breed's Hut when Thoreau was living at the edge of the village?
3. Who visited Thoreau that winter?

Chapter 15 – Winter Animals

Review Questions
1. Why did Thoreau feed the animals?
2. How did Thoreau explain the diligence of the foxhunting dogs?
3. What, according to Thoreau, were the two simplest and most indigenous (native) animals?

Chapter 16 – The Pond in Winter

Review Questions
1. What was Nature's resolution? Explain.
2. What did Thoreau want to recover? How did he do it? Why was he glad about his findings?
3. What did the landlords seek at Walden Pond in January?
4. How was the pond "revenged" on the takers, according to Thoreau?

Thought Questions
1. "If we knew all the laws of Nature, we should need only one fact...to infer all the particular results at that point." How close is science to achieving this goal?
2. Do you agree with Thoreau's description of ethics as "the law of averages"?

Chapter 17 – Spring

Review Questions
1. Why did the ice on Walden take longer to break up than that on other ponds?
2. Where in nature did Thoreau see the pattern of the leaf?
3. What inspired Thoreau to say, "There needs no stronger proof of immortality"?
4. When did Thoreau leave Walden Pond?

Chapter 18 – Conclusion

Review Questions
1. What are the arguments for traveling abroad versus exploring domestically?
2. Why did Thoreau leave the woods?
3. What accusation against his work did Thoreau fear?
4. What was Thoreau's response to the idea of "common sense"?
5. Why did the artist from Kouroo stay perennially young? What was the point of this story?

Thought Questions
1. Thoreau said, "The Universe is wider than our views of it." Explain. Do you agree?
2. Thoreau claimed that if you follow your dreams you are bound to succeed. Is this true?
3. Is it better to start with castles in the air or to build the foundations first?
4. Is a living dog better than a dead lion? Why or why not?
5. Thoreau said, "The fault-finder will find faults even in paradise." Did he mean this literally?
6. "The light which puts out our eyes is darkness to us…There is more day to dawn. The sun is but a morning star." Compare this quote to the end of 1 Corinthians 13. How are they similar?
7. Walden contains a number of religious overtones. Is it possible to take partial truth from someone's words, even if it is surrounded by untruths or misperceptions? Explain.

Brain Work
PREPARING AN OUTLINE

Imagine the thesis of your essay is that Thoreau's philosophy of simple living can be applied only in principle, not in practice.

Your main arguments are: 1) Thoreau depended heavily on the generosity of others for the success of his experiment, 2) If everyone tried to follow Thoreau's advice, society would never progress, and 3) Thoreau did not continue in that lifestyle after his two years at Walden Pond.

Your task is to lay out these arguments in an order that makes sense. For your outline, try to pick three main points and a few sub-points for each. Also, write out one-sentence transitions between each of the main points, making sure that there is a logical link between each section. If you find it difficult to create smooth transitions, consider going back and re-evaluating the order of your outline.

"On Self-Reliance"
Ralph W. Emerson

R alph Waldo Emerson (1803-1882) was born into a family of New England ministers, and he followed this path for several years, attending Harvard Divinity School before stepping away from the church. Emerson then spent several years traveling in Europe and studying naturalist philosophy. He later became a leader in the rising transcendentalist movement, an individualist American philosophy concerned with the relationship between the physical and the spiritual. Emerson's first two collections of essays, published in 1841 and 1844, discuss the fundamentals of this philosophy. Emerson was a poet as well as a philosopher, but he is best known for his essays. "On Self Reliance" was published as a part of the 1841 collection.

Note for Readers

Emerson's "Self Reliance" is one of the most densely packed readings in this book. Emerson is as much a philosopher as he is an author. Feel free to treat all of these questions as thought questions. After you understand what Emerson thinks about a given subject, take a minute to figure out what you think about it. One final encouragement: because Emerson is not easy reading, you will be able to understand his writing much better if you read it more than once. Skimming the essay will do you very little good, so read it slowly and carefully.

Review Questions
1. What, according to Emerson, is genius?
2. Every heart vibrates on what "iron string"?
3. What effect do babies have on the behavior of adults? What point is Emerson making?
4. What is the opposite of self-reliance?
5. What did Emerson say about virtues and good works? Why are they done?
6. What is the distinction between greatness and meanness?
7. What is the "foolish face of praise"?
8. Why is the anger of the masses harder to bear than that of the elite?

9. What is the foundation of self-reliance? Where does this source come from? Can we know?
10. What, for Emerson, was the highest truth on this subject?
11. What one fact does the world hate, and why?
12. From where did men get the power to annoy an individual, according to Emerson?
13. What is a true prayer? What is a false prayer?
14. What did Emerson say about traveling? About education? About society?
15. What did Emerson propose as an alternative to Fortune?

Thought Questions
1. Are the young truly free from outside influences? Can they judge neutrally? Explain.
2. What does it mean to have the name of goodness and not be good?
3. Emerson said, "The only right is what is after my constitution; the only wrong what is against it." If everyone lived by this principle, what would the world be like?
4. Is it acceptable for someone to fight against injustice if they are unjust in their personal life?
5. What is the value of community? Does being in community always imply conformity?
6. Are there any institutions that are not "the lengthened shadow of one man"?
7. Do we owe perfect faith to involuntary perceptions? Are they ever mistaken?
8. Emerson said that all relations with the Divine Spirit are in the present, not the past. What do you think he means when he speaks of a Divine Spirit?
9. Is there value in looking at the past? If so, what?
10. Emerson called power the measure of right. Do you agree?
11. Is there ever a situation in which it is appropriate to lie to those you love? If so, when?
12. Discuss the quote, "My giant goes with me wherever I go." Do you agree?
13. What do you think we lose as technology advances? Do the gains outweigh the losses?
14. Which of Emerson's precepts do you agree with or accept? Which do you reject? Why?
15. Does Emerson's philosophy sound like "the triumph of principles"? Why or why not?

Hand Work
FORMATTING CITATIONS

1. In each of these fictional citations (works cited or in-text), find and fix the mistakes in MLA format.

   James Brown. *History of Emerson*. Oxford UP: London, 1952.

   Grayson, Ellen. "Reading 'Self Reliance.'" Journal of 18th Century Philosophy. Vol. 22.3 (1992): 1-12.

   Emerson says, "Whoso would be a man must be a nonconformist." (page 134, R.W. Emerson).

2. Pretend you have written the following paragraph, but you want to insert quotes to support your argument. You have chosen three quotes, listed below, from "Self Reliance." Insert these quotes into the paragraph so it flows smoothly.[7] Be sure to use correct in-text citations. The works cited entry is:

   Emerson, Ralph Waldo. "Self Reliance." *The Selected Writings of Ralph Waldo Emerson*. Ed. Brooks Atkinson. New York: The Modern Library, 1992. 132-153.

   > "Life only avails, not the having lived." Page 144.

   > "Man postpones or remembers; he does not live in the present, but with reverted eye laments on these past [...] He cannot be happy and strong until he too lives with nature in the present." 143.

   > "Society never advances [...] The civilized man has built a coach, but has lost the use of his feet. He is supported on crutches, but lacks so much support of muscle." 151.

Paragraph

One of Emerson's most adamant points is his insistence that man should not depend on the past for information about how to live in the present. Emerson claims that by reflecting on the past, man misses out on life in the present. For Emerson, only the present is of value. Later, however, Emerson reflects on what has been lost as society has advanced. If Emerson truly put the past behind him, he could not base his explanation of modern society on what has been lost from the past. According to his philosophy, the present should speak for itself. However, Emerson has an easily prepared defense for this dilemma: great minds are not bound by the limits of consistency.

---

[7]Note: Three periods in a set of brackets [...]—called an ellipsis—indicates that a section of the quote has been removed. Whenever you quote selectively, you should use an ellipsis to indicate that part of the original quote has been cut.

The Old Man and the Sea
Ernest Hemingway

Ernest Miller Hemingway (1899-1961) was born in Illinois, where he entered the writing profession after high school as a newspaper writer. When World War I began, he was unable to serve as a soldier because of his poor eyesight, so instead he volunteered in an ambulance unit of the Red Cross in Italy, where he was wounded and earned a medal for valor. After the war, he continued to work as an international correspondent. Hemingway lived for several years in Paris among a group of expatriate writers including Ezra Pound and James Joyce. Later, he also spent time in Africa, Spain, and Cuba. As a writer of many successful short stories and novels, Hemingway became famous for his sparse writing style, and in 1954 he won a Nobel Prize in Literature. *The Old Man and the Sea* was published in Cuba in 1952, and won the Pulitzer Prize in 1953.

Review Questions
1. Why was the old man considered unlucky?
2. Why had the boy left Santiago?
3. Who was Santiago's favorite baseball player?
4. What was Santiago's most frequent dream?
5. How did Santiago use the man-of-war bird to fish?
6. What did Santiago feel on the fishing line? What was it doing? How could he tell?
7. What happened when Santiago tried to reel in the big fish?
8. Why did he think it was a male fish?
9. Why did Santiago want the fish to jump?
10. How big was the fish?
11. What was DiMaggio's weakness?
12. What had happened at the tavern in Casablanca?
13. Why couldn't Santiago fasten the line to the boat?
14. How did he know the fish was getting desperate?
15. What did Santiago have to do after he killed the fish?
16. What tracked the old man and the fish across the sea?
17. What did Santiago lose in defending the fish?

18. Santiago knew that there was "a very bad time coming." What did he mean?
19. What finally beat Santiago?
20. What was left of the fish at the end?

Thought Questions
1. Santiago said humility "carried no loss of true pride." What is true pride?
2. Why did the man and the boy carry on the fiction of the net and the pot of rice?
3. How did Santiago think of the sea? Why? How do you think of the sea?
4. Why do people talk to themselves? Is it a good thing or a bad thing?
5. Why is it important or symbolic that Santiago caught the fish "beyond all people in the world"?
6. Santiago caught the fish "far out beyond all snares and traps and treacheries." What did he mean?
7. Santiago wanted to show the fish "what sort of man" he was. What kind of man was he?
8. "It is enough to live on the sea and kill our true brothers." Explain.
9. Why did Santiago think the fish had a right to kill him?
10. "A man is not made for defeat. A man can be destroyed but not defeated." Do you agree?
11. Is it a sin not to hope? Discuss.
12. If Santiago loved the fish, was it more or less of a sin for him to kill it?
13. Can you buy luck?
14. Why do you think Santiago always dreamed of lions? What did his dreams mean?
15. Did Santiago win or lose in the end? Was he defeated? Why or why not?

Brain Work
CONDUCTING (primary) RESEARCH

When you write about literature, most of your research is primary research. Primary support takes the form of quotations from the book you are writing about.

Below is a sample outline for an essay on *The Old Man and the Sea*. For each of the first two main points, several quotes from the book are presented. Choose the quote that you think best supports the point. For the third heading, you must find a quote. Remember, this will be much easier if you took notes and marked quotes and page numbers as you read the book.

Thesis

In the story *The Old Man and the Sea*, the main character Santiago reflects on three things during his struggle with the fish: the tavern in Casablanca, his hero Joe DiMaggio, and his dream about the lion. Each of these reflections reveals something important about Santiago's character.

Outline

I. Introduction

II. Santiago's character traits

    A. Endurance (the tavern in Casablanca)

    "Many of the bettors had asked for a draw because they had to go to work on the docks loading sacks of sugar or at the Havana Coal Company […] But he had finished it anyway and before anyone had to go to work" (Hemingway 70).

    "They had gone one day and one night with their elbows on a chalk line on the table and their forearms straight up and their hands gripped tight" (69).

    B. Will (Joe DiMaggio)

    "I would like to take the great DiMaggio fishing,' the old man said. 'They say his father was a fisherman. Maybe he was as poor as we are and would understand'" (Hemingway 22).

    "Do you believe the great DiMaggio would stay with a fish as long as I will stay with this one? he thought. I am sure he would and more since he is young and strong" (68).

"I must be worthy of the great DiMaggio who does all things perfectly even with the pain of the bone spur in his heel" (68).

C. Pride (the dream about the lion)

(You find a quote to support this point)

III. Conclusion

Looking Back, Looking Forward

Congratulations! You have now worked your way through twenty-nine classic works of American literature. Along the way, you've assembled a variety of reading and thinking tools that will be valuable in future reading and writing experiences. So, you may be thinking, what now?

The Next Step

Almost every author says the key to good writing is lots and lots of reading. As a reader, you learn to pay attention to the techniques a writer uses. As writer, it's equally important to think about technique. One goal of this collection is to help you slow down and practice writing essays step-by-step.

As you continue to read and write about literature, always remember that you are first and foremost a critic. Books—even the most pleasurable—contain ideas, and it is your job to recognize those ideas and consider their implications. Whether you ultimately reject or accept an author's viewpoint, you cannot help being influenced by it.

For students in ninth to twelfth grade, or for learners of any age who are ready to ask questions and think analytically about literature, a great resource is *The Lost Tools of Writing* from the CiRCE Institute. Using the classical method, this guide will help you remove anxiety from the writing process.

Another resource to consider is the next book in the *Words Aptly Spoken* series, *Words Aptly Spoken: British Literature*. Through a study of classic works of British literature, this guide will help you think more deeply about the characteristics that make literature unique from other types of writing.

Both of these books build on the skills you've begun to hone and will help you continue your journey through the world of literature.

Perspectives, Take Two

In today's society, mass media has an enormous impact on the way people view the world. Every day a million and one ideas compete for your attention. Most messages are designed to be absorbed passively and accepted without questioning. If nothing else, this book encourages you to practice reading (and, by default, listening and watching) with your brain fully engaged. If you can do this, you will be better prepared to distinguish between that which is merely enjoyable and that which is worthy of application to your own life.

In closing, as you continue this journey, it's worth repeating that participating in the great conversations of literature is an art that takes a lifetime to refine. However, it is an art that will yield a lifetime of fruit as you celebrate with family and friends the joy of laughing, crying, and simply bubbling over with excitement about the great stories which are now yours to share.

Best wishes on your journey!

Photo Credits

The following images have been retrieved from the Library of Congress digital Prints and Photographs collection, unless otherwise noted. The reproduction number follows the photo description.

PAGES 73 and 79:
Longfellow, LC-USZ62-15635

PAGE 75:
"Awaken...," William Robinson Leigh, 1917, LC-USZ62-78305

PAGES 89 and 95:
Elizabeth George Speare, courtesy Houghton Mifflin Co.

PAGE 109:
Jack London, portrait photograph, LC-G3999-0049-E

PAGE 113:
Twain, Mark. LC-USZ62-5513

PAGE 121:
The late Louisa May Alcott. LC-USZ61-452

PAGE 127:
Herman Melville head-and-shoulders portrait, facing left. LC-USZ62-135949

PAGE 135:
Nathaniel Hawthorne, LC-USZ62-2358

PAGE 149:
Edgar Allan Poe, head-and-shoulders portrait, facing front. LC-USZ62-136223

PAGE 161:
Chuck Colson, courtesy Prison Fellowship Ministries.

PAGE 177:
Frederick Douglass, head-and-shoulders portrait, facing right. LC-USZ62-15887

PAGE 183:
Booker T. Washington, half-length portrait, seated. LC-J694-255

PAGE 193:
Harper Lee, half-length portrait, facing right, LC-USZ62-121597

PAGE 203:
Henry David Thoreau, head-and-shoulders portrait, facing slightly right. LC-USZ61-361

PAGE 211:
Ralph Waldo Emerson, 1803-1882. LC-USZ62-73430

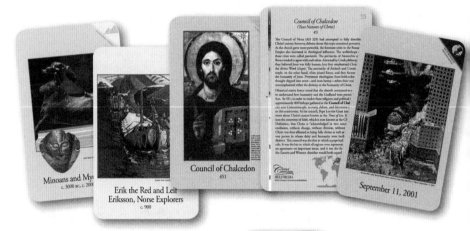

Transcript Services

Beginning in the ninth grade, parents must keep a record of students' classes and grades in a permanent high school transcript. Transcripts are necessary for high school diploma, college entrance, and college scholarship applications.

Classical Conversations can help! For a modest annual fee, our transcript service, AcademicRecords.net, provides transcripts, medical records, and resume information in a professionally-formatted report that you can print for your records or e-mail to appropriate college admissions or scholarship providers.

Please visit www.AcademicRecords.net to sign up.

To help organize your records...

Student Planner

The student planner provides a system to help parents instill a sense of schedule and discipline in their student's coursework. Begin using this in Foundations, and by the time students are in the upper Challenge levels, they will already have a system in place to help them organize the fuller course load, as well as an easy tool to compile transcript information.

Visit www.ClassicalConversationsBooks.com to purchase.

Testing Services

Parents of school-age children have several considerations when considering testing. Classical education, which focuses on the three stages of learning (grammar, dialectic, rhetoric), emphasizes test-taking skill development well beyond prescribing curriculum or courses of action based on results.

Any homeschool student, whether enrolled in a Classical Conversations community or not, may test with Homeschool Testing Services. We have been facilitating standardized testing for groups of homeschool students since 2008. In 2015, 10,000 students tested with us at 300 on-site locations and 70 online testing events. Well-qualified and experienced Test Coordinators and Proctors contract with us to provide you a relaxed and easy testing experience.

Ready to go to the next step? Get some great tips to prepare for testing.

Visit
HOMESCHOOLTESTINGSERVICES.COM
for hosted testing sites near you.

3-Day Parent Practicums

Each year, from May to July, Classical Conversations sponsors FREE one- and three-day Parent Practicums across the U.S.

Because parents are a child's first and best teachers, they are key to their children's academic success. Only Classical Conversations provides parents with the tools to help.

Knowing a topic well and being able to teach it aren't always the same thing. Also, people who truly love learning enjoy digging deeper and finding ways to share what they know with others.

Our Practicum materials are fun, innovative, and thought-provoking.

Plan to use your brain and laugh a lot! This is for parents and teachers of all grade levels desiring to practice teaching from a classical, Christian perspective.

Practicums are FREE, but space is limited, so registration is required. For information about Parent Practicums, visit the Equipping Events section of our website at www.ClassicalConversations.com. For dates and locations of Parent Practicums in your area, go to www.ClassicalConversations.com and click on the Event Calendar.

Now, three community tiers for your at-home learning

CHALLENGE

A classical, academic learning center designed to complement your classical, Christian community journey, at home. Parents have asked for more resources at home during the week that will help prepare for their weekly community conversation. Have you ever needed help with a Latin lesson? Help has arrived!

ESSENTIALS

Discover more about Essentials of the English Language through video tutorials in our Classical Learning Center: EEL section. Need a concise explanation of the five canons of rhetoric? See the writing section. For math drills you will find the complete text of *Tables, Squares & Cubes* page by page. In the Discussion Forum, find helpful user posts and conversations by thread, and in the File Sharing Center, parents (like you!) share helpful resources they have developed.

FOUNDATIONS

Our Classical Learning Center provides more general information about the Foundations program, as well as the *Classical Acts & Facts® History Card* timeline with hand motions. Engage with other Foundations parents in the Discussion Forum. The File Sharing Center lists extra resources that have been developed by parents—1,286 entries for Cycle 2 alone! Finally, the Online Tutorials provide interactive memory work tutorials for Cycles 1, 2, and 3 with audio for extra memory work practice. Updated tutorials are in HTML5, which allows for mobile device access.

Community members receive substantial discounts for membership. Plus, when you register (which is free), there is a FREE guest area with previews and resources.